LABORATORY MANUAL

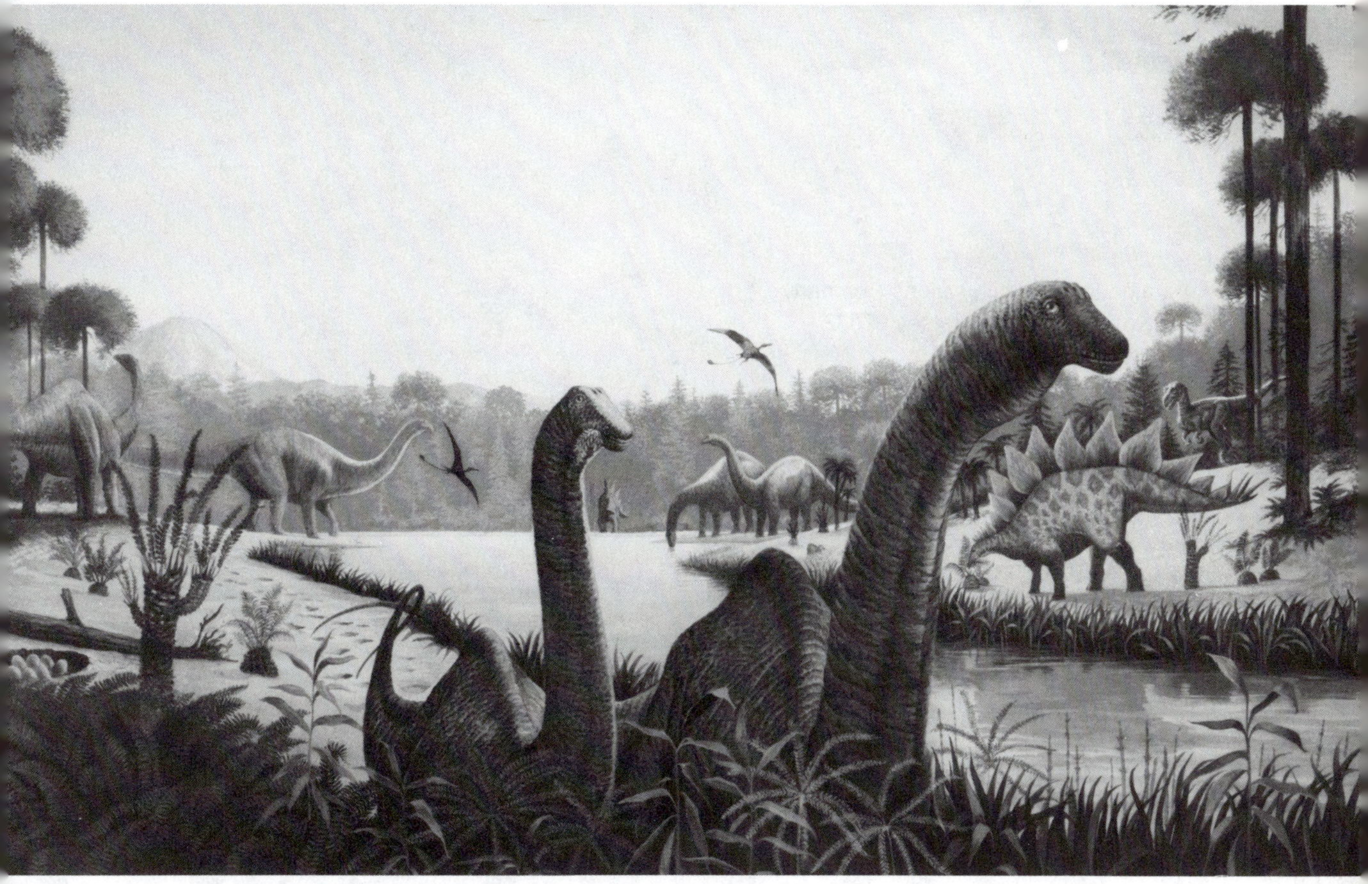

Prentice Hall
Englewood Cliffs, New Jersey
Needham, Massachusetts

Laboratory Manual

PRENTICE HALL
Exploring Earth Science

ISBN 0-13-807645-6

3 4 5 6 7 8 9 10 98 97 96

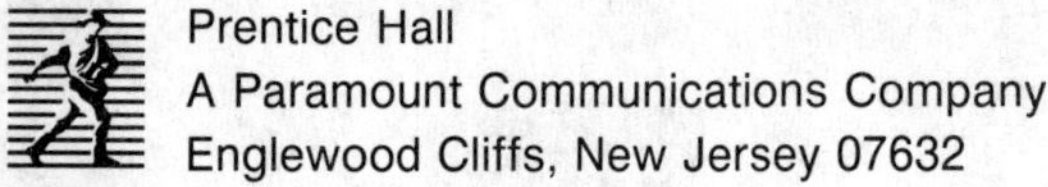

Contents

Safety Symbols 6
Science Safety Rules 7
Laboratory Skills Checkups 9

CHAPTER 1 ■ *Exploring Earth Science*

1 Metric Measurement: Length 17
2 Metric Measurement: Mass 21

CHAPTER 2 ■ *Stars and Galaxies*

3 Comparing Chemical Composition and the Spectrum 25
4 Measuring the Diameter of the Sun 29

CHAPTER 3 ■ *The Solar System*

5 Characteristics of Elliptical Orbits 33
6 Relating Gravitational Force and Orbits 37
7 Relating Distance and Apparent Motion 41

CHAPTER 4 ■ *Earth and Its Moon*

8 Constructing a Foucault Pendulum 45
9 Comparing the Angle of Insolation and Temperature Changes 49
10 Models of Eclipses 53

CHAPTER 5 ■ *Earth's Atmosphere*

11 Finding the Percentage of Oxygen in the Atmosphere 57
12 Effect of the Atmosphere on Cooling Rates of the Earth's Surface 61

CHAPTER 6 ■ *Earth's Oceans*

13 Relating Salinity and Density 65
14 Culturing and Observing Brine Shrimp 69
15 Investigating Density Currents 75

CHAPTER 7 ■ *Earth's Fresh Water*

16 Investigating Porosity and Permeability 81
17 Examining the Pollution of a Water Supply 85

CHAPTER 8 ■ *Earth's Landmasses*

18 Constructing a Topographic Map 89
19 Using a Topographic Map 93

CHAPTER 9 ■ *Earth's Interior*

20 Observing the Action of Gases in a Magma 97
21 Determining the Density of the Earth 101
22 A Model of the Earth's Interior 105

CHAPTER 10 ■ *Movement of the Earth's Crust*

23 Examining Faulting and Folding 109

CHAPTER 11 ■ *Earthquakes and Volcanoes*

24 Locating an Epicenter 113
25 Investigating the Speed of Earthquake Waves 119

CHAPTER 12 ■ *Plate Tectonics*

26 Observing Convection Currents 123

CHAPTER 13 ■ *Rocks and Minerals*

27 Identifying Common Minerals 127
28 Calculating the Specific Gravity of Minerals 133
29 Classifying Rocks 137
30 Relating Cooling Rate and Crystal Size 143

CHAPTER 14 ■ *Weathering and Soil Formation*

31 Investigating Rock Abrasion 147
32 Observing the Effects of Chemical Weathering on Chalk 151
33 Investigating the Composition of Soil 155
34 A Closer Look at Soil 159

CHAPTER 15 ■ *Erosion and Deposition*

35 Using a Stream Table 163
36 Observing Sediment Deposition in Quiet Water 169

CHAPTER 16 ■ *What Is Weather?*

37 Constructing a Barometer for Observing Changes in Air Pressure 173
38 Investigating Weather Maps 177

CHAPTER 17 ■ *What Is Climate?*

39 Investigating Differences in Climate 185

CHAPTER 18 ■ *Climate in the United States*

40 Adaptations of Plants in Different Biomes 191

CHAPTER 19 ■ *Earth's History in Fossils*

41 Interpreting Events From Fossil Evidence 195
42 Interpreting a Sediment Deposition Model 199
43 Using the Rock Record to Interpret Geologic History 205
44 Demonstrating Half-Life 209

CHAPTER 20 ■ *A Trip Through Geologic Time*

45 Exploring Geologic Time Through Sediment "Core" Samples 213

CHAPTER 21 ■ *Energy Resources*

46 Fractional Distillation 217

CHAPTER 22 ■ *Earth's Nonliving Resources*

47 An Experiment in Hydroponics 221

CHAPTER 23 ■ *Pollution*

48 Investigating the Effects of Pollution on Germination 225
49 The Greenhouse Effect 229
50 Observing Oil Spills 233
51 Treating Polluted Water 237

CHAPTER 24 ■ *Conserving Earth's Resources*

52 Should You Take a Bath or a Shower? 241

Safety Symbols

All the investigations in this *Laboratory Manual* have been designed with safety in mind. If you follow the instructions, you should have a safe and interesting year in the laboratory. Before beginning any investigation, make sure you read the safety rules that follow.

The eight safety symbols below appear next to certain steps in some of the investigations in this *Laboratory Manual*. The symbols alert you to the need for special safety precautions. The description of each symbol below tells you which precautions to take whenever you see the symbol in an investigation.

Glassware Safety

1. Whenever you see this symbol, you will know that you are working with glassware that can easily be broken. Take particular care to handle such glassware safely. And never use broken or chipped glassware.
2. Never heat glassware that is not thoroughly dry. Never pick up any glassware unless you are sure it is not hot. If it is hot, use heat-resistant gloves.
3. Always clean glassware thoroughly before putting it away.

Fire Safety

1. Whenever you see this symbol, you will know that you are working with fire. Never use any source of fire without wearing safety goggles.
2. Never heat anything—particularly chemicals—unless instructed to do so.
3. Never heat anything in a closed container.
4. Never reach across a flame.
5. Always use a clamp, tongs, or heat-resistant gloves to handle hot objects.
6. Always maintain a clean work area, particularly when using a flame.

Heat Safety

Whenever you see this symbol, you will know that you should put on heat-resistant gloves to avoid burning your hands.

Chemical Safety

1. Whenever you see this symbol, you will know that you are working with chemicals that could be hazardous.
2. Never smell any chemical directly from its container. Always use your hand to waft some of the odors from the top of the container toward your nose—and only when instructed to do so.
3. Never mix chemicals unless instructed to do so.
4. Never touch or taste any chemical unless instructed to do so.
5. Keep all lids closed when chemicals are not in use. Dispose of all chemicals as instructed by your teacher.
6. Immediately rinse with water any chemicals, particularly acids, that get on your skin and clothes. Then notify your teacher.

Eye and Face Safety

1. Whenever you see this symbol, you will know that you are performing an experiment in which you must take precautions to protect your eyes and face by wearing safety goggles.
2. When you are heating a test tube or bottle, always point it away from you and others. Chemicals can splash or boil out of a heated test tube.

Sharp Instrument Safety

1. Whenever you see this symbol, you will know that you are working with a sharp instrument.
2. Always use single-edged razors; double-edged razors are too dangerous.
3. Handle any sharp instrument with extreme care. Never cut any material toward you; always cut away from you.
4. Immediately notify your teacher if your skin is cut.

Electrical Safety

1. Whenever you see this symbol, you will know that you are using electricity in the laboratory.
2. Never use long extension cords to plug in any electrical device. Do not plug too many appliances into one socket or you may overload the socket and cause a fire.
3. Never touch an electrical appliance or outlet with wet hands.

Animal Safety

1. Whenever you see this symbol, you will know that you are working with live animals.
2. Do not cause pain, discomfort, or injury to an animal.
3. Follow your teacher's directions when handling animals. Wash your hands thoroughly after handling animals or their cages.

Science Safety Rules

One of the first things a scientist learns is that working in the laboratory can be an exciting experience. But the laboratory can also be quite dangerous if proper safety rules are not followed at all times. To prepare yourself for a safe year in the laboratory, read over the following safety rules. Then read them a second time. Make sure you understand each rule. If you do not, ask your teacher to explain any rules you are unsure of.

Dress Code

1. Many materials in the laboratory can cause eye injury. To protect yourself from possible injury, wear safety goggles whenever you are working with chemicals, burners, or any substance that might get into your eyes. Never wear contact lenses in the laboratory.
2. Wear a laboratory apron or coat whenever you are working with chemicals or heated substances.
3. Tie back long hair to keep it away from any chemicals, burners, and candles, or other laboratory equipment.
4. Remove or tie back any article of clothing or jewelry that can hang down and touch chemicals and flames.

General Safety Rules

5. Read all directions for an experiment several times. Follow the directions exactly as they are written. If you are in doubt about any part of the experiment, ask your teacher for assistance.
6. Never perform activities that are not authorized by your teacher. Obtain permission before "experimenting" on your own.
7. Never handle any equipment unless you have specific permission.
8. Take extreme care not to spill any material in the laboratory. If a spill occurs, immediately ask your teacher about the proper cleanup procedure. Never simply pour chemicals or other substances into the sink or trash container.
9. Never eat in the laboratory.
10. Wash your hands before and after each experiment.

First Aid

11. Immediately report all accidents, no matter how minor, to your teacher.
12. Learn what to do in case of specific accidents, such as getting acid in your eyes or on your skin. (Rinse acids from your body with lots of water.)
13. Become aware of the location of the first-aid kit. But your teacher should administer any required first aid due to injury. Or your teacher may send you to the school nurse or call a physician.
14. Know where and how to report an accident or fire. Find out the location of the fire extinguisher, phone, and fire alarm. Keep a list of important phone numbers—such as the fire department and the school nurse—near the phone. Immediately report any fires to your teacher.

Heating and Fire Safety

15. Again, never use a heat source, such as a candle or a burner, without wearing safety goggles.
16. Never heat a chemical you are not instructed to heat. A chemical that is harmless when cool may be dangerous when heated.
17. Maintain a clean work area and keep all materials away from flames.
18. Never reach across a flame.
19. Make sure you know how to light a Bunsen burner. (Your teacher will demonstrate the proper procedure for lighting a burner.) If the flame leaps out of a burner toward you, immediately turn off the gas. Do not touch the burner. It may be hot. And never leave a lighted burner unattended!
20. When heating a test tube or bottle, always point it away from you and others. Chemicals can splash or boil out of a heated test tube.

21. Never heat a liquid in a closed container. The expanding gases produced may blow the container apart, injuring you or others.
22. Before picking up a container that has been heated, first hold the back of your hand near it. If you can feel the heat on the back of your hand, the container may be too hot to handle. Use a clamp or tongs when handling hot containers.

Using Chemicals Safely

23. Never mix chemicals for the "fun of it." You might produce a dangerous, possibly explosive substance.
24. Never touch, taste, or smell a chemical unless you are instructed by your teacher to do so. Many chemicals are poisonous. If you are instructed to note the fumes in an experiment, gently wave your hand over the opening of a container and direct the fumes toward your nose. Do not inhale the fumes directly from the container.
25. Use only those chemicals needed in the activity. Keep all lids closed when a chemical is not being used. Notify your teacher whenever chemicals are spilled.
26. Dispose of all chemicals as instructed by your teacher. To avoid contamination, never return chemicals to their original containers.
27. Be extra careful when working with acids or bases. Pour such chemicals over the sink, not over your workbench.
28. When diluting an acid, pour the acid into water. Never pour water into the acid.
29. Immediately rinse with water any acids that get on your skin or clothing. Then notify your teacher of any acid spill.

Using Glassware Safely

30. Never force glass tubing into a rubber stopper. A turning motion and lubricant will be helpful when inserting glass tubing into rubber stoppers or rubber tubing. Your teacher will demonstrate the proper way to insert glass tubing.
31. Never heat glassware that is not thoroughly dry. Use a wire screen to protect glassware from any flame.
32. Keep in mind that hot glassware will not appear hot. Never pick up glassware without first checking to see if it is hot. See #22.
33. If you are instructed to cut glass tubing, fire-polish the ends immediately to remove sharp edges.
34. Never use broken or chipped glassware. If glassware breaks, notify your teacher and dispose of the glassware in the proper trash container.
35. Never eat or drink from laboratory glassware.
36. Thoroughly clean glassware before putting it away.

Using Sharp Instruments

37. Handle scalpels or razor blades with extreme care. Never cut material toward you; cut away from you.
38. Immediately notify your teacher if you cut your skin when working in the laboratory.

Animal Safety

39. No experiments that cause pain, discomfort, or harm to mammals, birds, reptiles, fish, and amphibians should be done in the classroom or at home.
40. Animals should be handled only if necessary. If an animal is excited or frightened, pregnant, feeding, or with its young, special handling is required.
41. Your teacher will instruct you as to how to handle each animal species that may be brought into the classroom.
42. Clean your hands thoroughly after handling animals or the cage containing animals.

End-of-Experiment Rules

43. After an experiment has been completed, clean up your work area and return all equipment to its proper place.
44. Wash your hands after every experiment.
45. Turn off all candles and burners before leaving the laboratory. Check that the gas line leading to the burner is off as well.

Name ______________________ Class ____________ Date ________

Laboratory Skills Checkup 1

Following Directions

1. Read all of the following directions before you do anything.
2. Print your name, last name first then your first name and middle initial (if you have one), at the top of this page.
3. Draw a line through the word "all" in direction 1.
4. Underline the word "directions" in direction 1.
5. In direction 2, circle the words "your first name."
6. In direction 3, place an "X" in front of the word "through."
7. Cross out the numbers of the even-numbered directions above.
8. In direction 7, cross out the word "above" and write the word "below" above it.
9. Write "Following directions is easy" under your name at the top of this page.
10. In direction 9, add the following sentence after the word "page." "That's what you think!"
11. Draw a square in the upper right-hand corner of this page.
12. Draw a triangle in the lower left-hand corner of this page.
13. Place a circle in the center of the square.
14. Place an "X" in the center of the triangle.
15. Now that you have read all the directions as instructed in direction 1, follow directions 2 and 16 only.
16. Please do not give away what this test is about by saying anything or doing anything to alert your classmates. If you have reached this direction, make believe you are still writing. See how many of your classmates really know how to follow directions.

Name ______________________________ Class ______________ Date ________

Laboratory Skills Checkup 2

Defining Elements of a Scientific Method

Laboratory activities and experiments involve the use of the scientific method. Listed in the left column are the names of parts of this method. The right column contains definitions. Next to each word in the left column, write the letter of the definition that best matches.

Objective	A. Proposed explanation for a problem or observation
Research	B. Problem that the laboratory activity is designed to solve
Hypothesis	C. Measurements
Variable	D. Result of a laboratory activity
Control	E. Factor being tested
Observation	F. What the person performing the activity sees, hears, feels, smells, or tastes
Data	G. Experiment with the variable left out
Conclusion	H. Gathering information about the subject of the activity

Name ____________________ Class __________ Date __________

Laboratory Skills Checkup 3

Analyzing Elements of a Scientific Method

Read the following statements and then answer the questions.

1. You and your friend are walking along a beach in Alaska on January 15, 1995, at 8:00 AM.
2. You notice a thermometer on a nearby building that reads −1°C.
3. You also notice that there is snow on the roof of the building and icicles hanging from the roof.
4. You further notice a pool of sea water in the sand near the ocean.
5. Your friend looks at the icicles and the pool and says, "How come the water on the roof is frozen and the sea water is not?"
6. You answer, "I think that the salt in the sea water keeps it from freezing at −1°C."
7. You go on to say, "And I think under the same conditions, the same thing will happen tomorrow."
8. Your friend asks, "How can you be sure?" You answer, "I'm going to get some fresh water and some salt water and expose them to a temperature of −1°C and see what happens."

Questions

A. In which statement is a **prediction** made? ____________________

B. Which statement states a **problem**? ____________________

C. In which statement is an **experiment** described? ____________________

D. Which statement contains a **hypothesis**? ____________________

E. Which statements contain **data**? ____________________

F. In which statement is an **objective** mentioned? ____________________

G. Which statements describe **observations**? ____________________

Name ______________________ Class ____________ Date ________

Laboratory Skills Checkup 4

Performing an Experiment

Read the following statements and then answer the questions.

1. A scientist wants to find out why sea water freezes at a lower temperature than fresh water.

2. The scientist goes to the library and reads a number of articles about the physical properties of solutions.

3. The scientist also reads about the composition of sea water.

4. The scientist travels to a nearby beach and observes the conditions there. The scientist notes the taste of the sea water and other factors such as waves, wind, air pressure, temperature, and humidity.

5. After considering all this information, the scientist sits at a desk and writes, "My guess is that sea water freezes at a lower temperature than fresh water because sea water has salt in it."

6. The scientist goes back to the laboratory and does the following:
a. Fills each of two beakers with 1 liter of fresh water.
b. Dissolves 35 grams of table salt in one of the beakers.
c. Places both beakers in a refrigerator whose temperature is −1°C
d. Leaves the beakers in the refrigerator for 24 hours

7. After 24 hours, the scientist examines both beakers and finds the fresh water to be frozen. The salt water is still liquid.

8. The scientist writes in a notebook, "It appears as if salt water freezes at a lower temperature than fresh water does."

9. The scientist continues, "Therefore, I suggest that the reason sea water freezes at a lower temperature is that sea water contains dissolved salts while fresh water does not."

Questions

A. Which statements contain **conclusions**? ______________________

B. Which statements refer to **research**? ______________________

C. Which statement contains a **hypothesis**? ______________________

D. Which statements contain **observations**? ______________________

E. Which statements describe an **experiment**? ______________________

Name ______________________ Class ____________ Date ________

F. Which statement **supports** the **hypothesis**? ______________________

G. In which statement is the **problem** defined? ______________________

H. Which statements contain **data**? ______________________

I. Which is the **variable** in the experiment? ______________________

J. What is the **control** in the experiment? ______________________

K. Which statement includes an **inference**? ______________________

Name ______________________ Class ____________ Date ________

Laboratory Skills Checkup 5

Identifying Errors

Read the following paragraph and then answer the questions.

George arrived at school and went directly to his earth science class. He took off his cap and coat and sat down at his desk. His teacher gave him a large rock and asked him to find its density. Realizing that the rock was too large to work with, George got a hammer from the supply cabinet and hit the rock several times until he broke off a chip small enough to work with. George partly filled a graduated cylinder with water and suspended the rock in the water. The water level rose 2 centimeters. George committed this measurement to memory. George next weighed the rock on a balance. The rock weighed 4 ounces. George then calculated the density of the rock as follows: He divided 2 centimeters by 4 ounces. He then reported to his teacher that the density of the rock was .5 centimeter/ounce.

Questions

1. What safety rule did George break? ______________________

____

2. What mistake did George make in using the graduated cylinder? ______________________

____

3. What should George have done with his data rather than committing them to memory? ______

____

4. What is wrong with the statement "George next weighed the rock on a balance"? ______

____

5. Why is "4 ounces" an inappropriate measurement? ______________________

6. What mistake did George make in calculating density? ______________________

____

Name ______________________ Class __________ Date __________

Laboratory Skills Checkup 6

Making Measurements

Look at the drawings and write the letter of the drawing next to the description that it matches.

1. Measures time ______________
2. Measures mineral hardness ______________
3. Measures mass ______________
4. Measures volume ______________
5. Measures air pressure ______________
6. Measures temperature ______________
7. Measures earthquake waves ______________
8. Measures length ______________

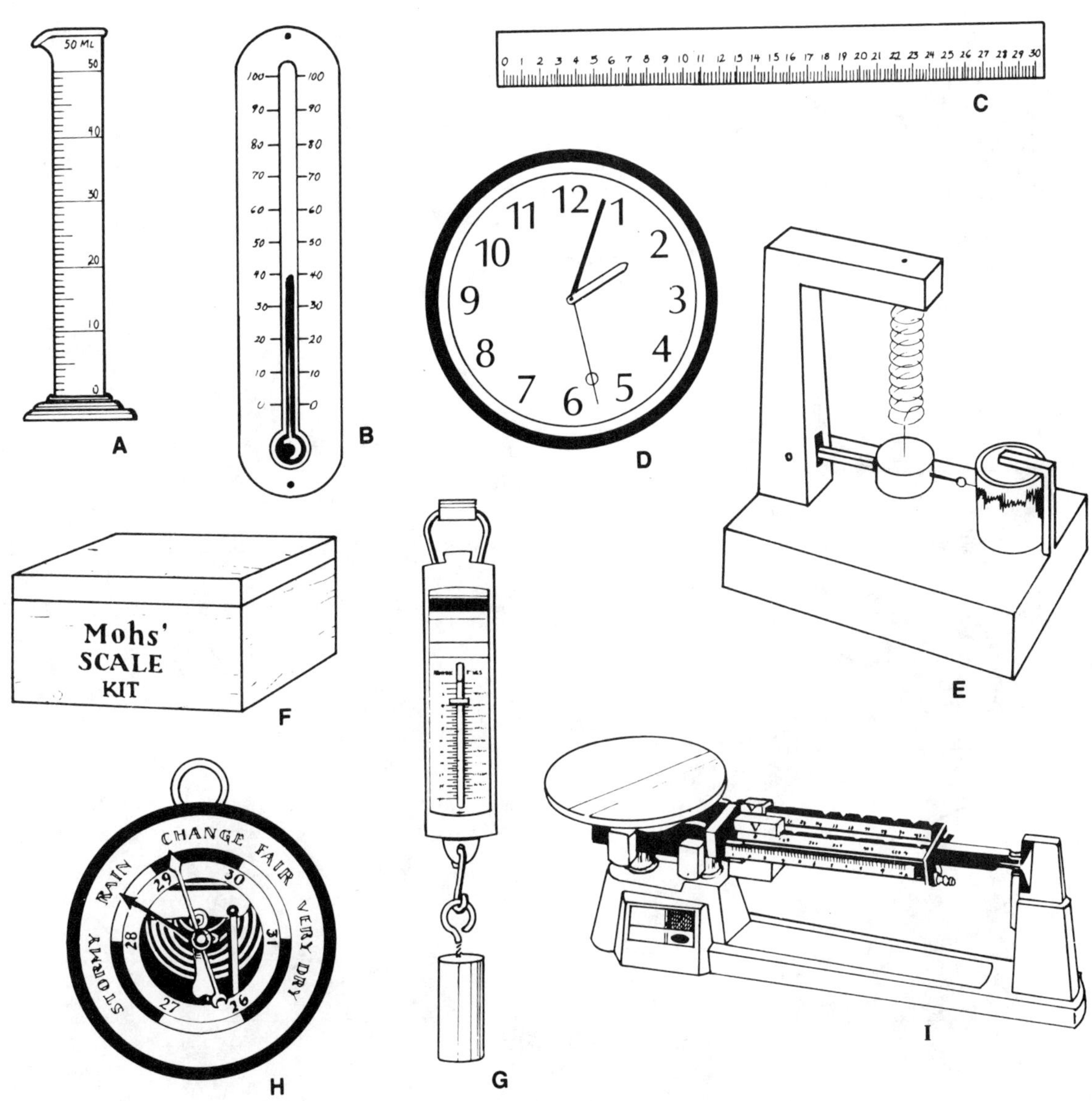

Name ______________________ Class ____________ Date ________

Laboratory Skills Checkup 7

Safety First

Circle any drawing that shows an unsafe laboratory activity and explain why it is unsafe.

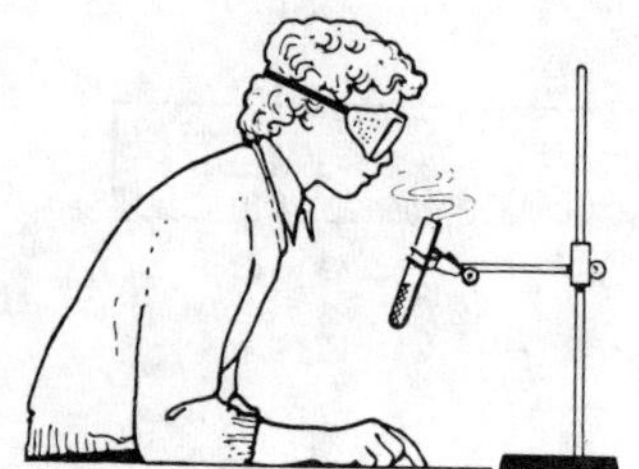

Name ____________________ Class ____________ Date ________

Laboratory Investigation

Chapter 1 Exploring Earth Science **1**

Metric Measurement: Length

Background Information

Length, or linear distance, is measured in the metric system in meters. Some objects are too small to be measured in meters, so scientists use centimeters (1/100 of a meter) or millimeters (1/1000 of a meter) to express these measurements. Each metric unit is 10 times larger or 10 times smaller than the next unit. The laboratory equipment used for measuring linear distances is the meterstick or metric ruler.

In this investigation you will learn how to accurately measure linear distance and express the measurement in the proper metric unit.

Problem

What is the proper way to use the meterstick and metric ruler to measure linear distances of different objects?

Materials *(per group)*

meterstick
metric ruler
1-m piece of string
pen
pencil
test tube

Procedure

1. With the meterstick or metric ruler, make the measurements of the various objects listed in Data Table 1. Record your measurements to the nearest centimeter in Data Table 1.

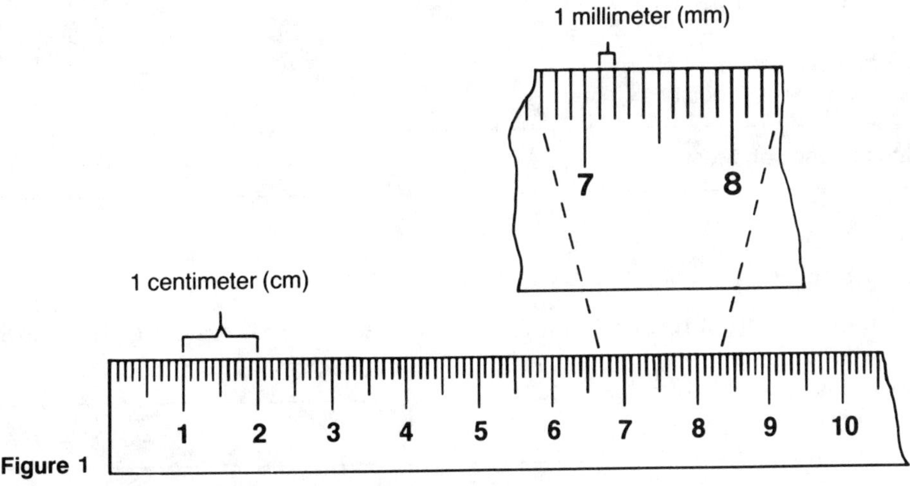

Figure 1

2. Convert the measurements from centimeters to meters and then to millimeters. Record these measurements in Data Table 1.

3. Now make the measurements listed in Data Table 2. To measure the distance around a circular object, or its circumference, wrap the piece of string around the object, keeping one end fixed. With the pen, make a mark on the string where the free end touches the fixed end of the string.

4. Remove the string and measure its length with a metric ruler or a meterstick. Record your measurement to the nearest centimeter, meter, and millimeter in Data Table 2.

Observations

DATA TABLE 1

	Centimeters (cm)	Meters (m)	Millimeters (mm)
Length of chalkboard			
Width of chalkboard			
Length of bulletin board			
Width of bulletin board			
Length of lab table			
Width of lab table			
Height of lab table			
Height of classroom door			

DATA TABLE 2

	Centimeters (cm)	Meters (m)	Millimeters (mm)
Circumference of your wrist			
Circumference of your lower arm at its widest point			
Circumference of your upper arm at its widest point			
Circumference of a test tube			

Analysis and Conclusions

1. Is the meter, centimeter, or millimeter more useful for measuring the length and width of your classroom? Why? ______________________________

____

____

____

Name ______________________ Class ____________ Date ________

2. Which metric unit would you use to measure the thickness of a nickel? Why?

____

____

____

3. a. How many millimeters are there in 1 m? ______________________

b. How many centimeters are there in 1 m? ______________________

4. a. How do you convert meters to centimeters? Centimeters to millimeters?

____

____

b. How do you convert millimeters to centimeters? Centimeters to meters?

____

____

____

Critical Thinking and Application

1. Why is it easier to convert meters to centimeters or millimeters than it is to change yards to feet or inches? ______________________

____

____

____

____

2. Using a metric ruler, student X measured the length of an object to the nearest tenth (0.1) of a centimeter while student Y measured its length to the nearest centimeter.

Which measurement is more accurate? ______________________

____

____

____

3. Explain how you might set up your own system of measurement using a length of string. Refer to your metric unit of measurement as an arak.

___

___

___

4. Suppose you were given a length of string and an irregularly shaped piece from a jigsaw puzzle. How would you determine the perimeter of the piece of the jigsaw puzzle? (Perimeter is the distance around the outside edge of an object.)

___

___

___

___

Going Further

Measure the thickness and circumference of a nickel and the length and circumference of your pencil and index finger. Which metric tool did you use, meterstick or metric ruler? Explain. Which unit of measurement did you use? Explain.

Laboratory Investigation

Metric Measurement: Mass

Background Information

The ability to accurately measure the mass of an object is an important skill in the earth science laboratory. The triple-beam balance is the instrument most frequently used to measure the mass of an object. There are three ways in which the triple-beam balance may be used to measure mass.

1. *Measuring mass directly:* The object is placed on the pan of the balance and the riders are moved into position on the beams until the pointer is balanced at the zero point. The mass is determined by the positions of the riders on the beams.
2. *Finding mass by difference:* This procedure is most frequently used to find the mass of a liquid in a container. The mass of the empty container is subtracted from the combined mass of the container and the liquid.
3. *Measuring out a substance:* It is necessary to use this procedure to obtain an exact amount of a solid chemical substance. Chemicals should never be placed directly on the balance pan, so it is necessary to first find the mass of the weighing paper or container. Add this amount to the desired mass of the chemical, and preset the riders to this number. The chemical is then added to the paper a little at a time until the pointer is balanced at the zero point.

In this investigation you will learn how to accurately measure the mass of various objects using the three methods described above.

Problem

What is the proper way to use the triple-beam balance to measure the mass of different objects?

Materials *(per group)*

triple-beam balance
100-mL graduated cylinder
coin
large paper clip
rubber stopper
weighing paper
small scoop
table salt
250-mL beaker

Procedure

Before beginning, be sure that the riders are moved all the way to the left and that the pointer rests on zero. See Figure 1.

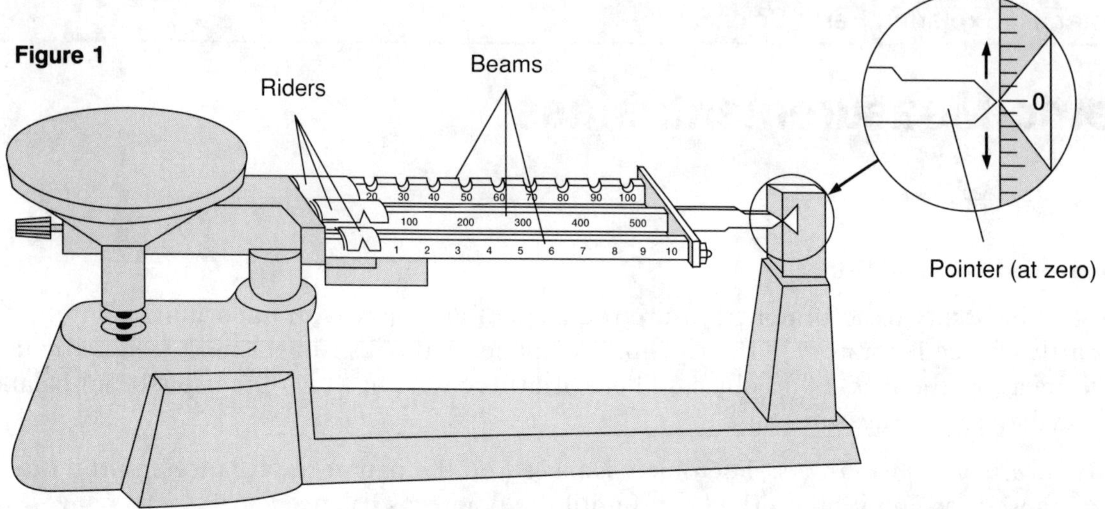

Part A Measuring Mass Directly

1. Place the coin on the pan of the balance.
2. Move the rider on the middle beam one notch at a time until the pointer drops below zero. Move the rider back one notch.
3. Move the rider on the back beam one notch at a time until the pointer again drops below zero. Move the rider back one notch.
4. Slide the rider along the front beam until the pointer stops at zero. The mass of the object is equal to the sum of the readings on the three beams.
5. Record the mass to the nearest tenth of a gram in Data Table 1.
6. Remove the coin and repeat steps 2 through 5 using the paper clip and then the rubber stopper.

Part B Finding Mass by Difference

1. Find the mass of an empty 250-mL beaker. Record the mass in Data Table 2.
2. Using the graduated cylinder, obtain 50 mL of water.
3. Pour the water into the beaker and find the mass of the beaker and water. Record the mass in Data Table 2.

Part C Measuring Out a Substance

1. Place a piece of weighing paper on the balance pan and find its mass. Record the mass in Data Table 3.
2. Add exactly 5 g to the value of the mass of the weighing paper and move the riders to this number.
3. Obtain a sample of table salt from your teacher. Using the scoop, add a small amount of salt at a time to the paper on the balance pan until the pointer rests on zero.
4. Dispose of the table salt in the container provided by your teacher.

Name ______________________ Class ____________ Date ________

Observations

DATA TABLE 1

Object	Mass (g)
Coin	
Paper clip	
Rubber stopper	

DATA TABLE 2

Mass of Empty Beaker (g)	Mass of Beaker With 50 mL of Water (g)

DATA TABLE 3

Mass of Weighing Paper (g)	Mass of Weighing Paper and Table Salt (g)

Analysis and Conclusions

1. What is the mass of 50 mL of water? ______________________

2. Which rider on the balance should always be moved first when finding the mass of an object? ______________________

____

____

3. What is the mass of the largest object your balance is able to measure? ____________

4. What is the mass of the smallest object your balance is able to measure accurately?

____

5. After using your balance, how should it always be left? ______________________

____

____

Critical Thinking and Application

1. In this lab, you found the mass of 50 mL of water. Calculate the mass of 1 mL of water. (Do not use the balance.) ______

2. Describe how you could find the mass of a certain quantity of milk that you poured into a drinking glass. ______

3. If you were baking a cake and the recipe called for 250 g of sugar, how would you use the triple-beam balance to obtain this amount? ______

Going Further

If other types of laboratory balances are available, such as a centigram balance or a double-pan balance, use them to find the mass of different objects. Compare the accuracy of the different balances.

Comparing Chemical Composition and the Spectrum

Background Information

Scientists can learn about stars and other bodies in space by studying the spectrum, or component colors, of the light these objects give off. When substances are heated, they give off light of different colors. A spectroscope is a device that breaks light into its component colors. By using a spectroscope to examine the light an object gives off, the chemical composition of the substance can be determined.

In this investigation you will use a spectroscope to examine the spectra of several different substances and then determine the chemical composition of an unknown sample.

Problem

How can astronomers learn about distant stars?

Materials *(per group)*

hand-held spectroscope
4 nichrome wire test loops
samples of calcium chloride, strontium chloride, potassium chloride, and sodium chloride
Bunsen burner or alcohol burner
safety goggles
colored pencils

Procedure

1. Light and adjust the burner to give a hot, blue flame.
2. Look at the flame through the spectroscope. The slit of the spectroscope should be vertical. The eyepiece should be rotated to provide a sharp spectrum on the side wall of the spectroscope.
3. While you are looking at the flame through the spectroscope, have one of your groupmates carefully dip the nichrome wire into the sample of calcium chloride and place the sample in the flame. In the space below, draw what you see through the spectroscope as the sample glows. Use colored pencils or label the colors that you see. Trade places with your groupmates and allow each group member to observe the spectrum of calcium chloride.

Spectrum of Calcium Chloride

4. Repeat step 3 with the samples of sodium chloride, potassium chloride, and strontium chloride. **Note:** *Be sure to use a separate nichrome wire loop for each substance.* Draw the spectrum for each substance in the spaces provided below.

Spectrum of Sodium Chloride

Spectrum of Potassium Chloride

Spectrum of Strontium Chloride

5. When you have finished, obtain a sample of the unknown substance from your teacher. Repeat step 3. Observe and record the spectrum of the unknown sample in the space below.

Spectrum of Unknown

Observations

1. How did the spectra of the samples differ?

____

2. If all the bands you observed were drawn on one band, what would it look like?

____

____

Analysis and Conclusions

1. What might the unknown sample contain? How do you know?

____

____

2. How can scientists tell what substances may be in a distant star?

____

3. Why must you use a separate nichrome wire loop for each substance?

____

____

Critical Thinking and Application

1. How do the samples resemble stars? ______________________

____

2. What other device besides a spectroscope breaks light into its component colors?

____

3. Spectral lines are often called the "fingerprints" of the elements. Why do you think this is so? ______________________

____

____

4. Why do you think these compounds give off light having a characteristic spectrum when they are heated? ______________________

____

____

____

____

Going Further

1. Observe the spectra of light from 25-watt, 40-watt, 60-watt, and 100-watt light bulbs. How do the spectra differ? How can scientists determine the temperature of a distant star by using a spectroscope?
2. Have you ever noticed how a train whistle or ambulance siren sounds different when it is coming toward you than when it is going away from you? The spectrum of light looks different when the light source is coming toward you or going away from you. This is known as the Doppler effect. Using one of the light bulbs, have your partner move it toward you as you observe it through the spectroscope. Then have your partner move it away from you. What changes do you notice? How can scientists determine if a distant star is coming toward the Earth or going away from it?

Laboratory Investigation

Chapter 2 Stars and Galaxies **4**

Measuring the Diameter of the Sun

Background Information

Even though the Earth is nearly 150,000,000 km from the sun at its closest approach, it is still possible to make accurate measurements of the sun's size by using instruments. In this investigation you will construct a simple device and use it to collect data that will allow you to calculate the diameter of the sun.

Problem

What is the diameter of the sun and how can it be determined?

Materials *(per group)*

meterstick
card, 20 cm × 25 cm
card, 10 cm × 15 cm
scissors
tape
small square piece of aluminum foil
drawing compass or pin
single-edged razor blade

Procedure

1. Use the razor blade to carefully cut slits in each card in the positions shown in Figure 1 so that the meterstick can fit through them. Cut each slit in the form of a capital "I." Make the openings small enough so that the meterstick fits tightly.
2. Draw two parallel lines exactly 0.8 cm apart near the center of the small card as shown in Figure 1.
3. Cut a large square hole in the larger card and cover it with aluminum foil. Use tape to hold the foil securely in place. Punch a very small hole near the center of the foil with a compass point or a pin.
4. Place the large card near one end of the meterstick and tape it in place. Be careful to fasten it so that it is perpendicular to the meterstick. Place the small card on the other end. For best results, the cards must be kept perpendicular to the meterstick.

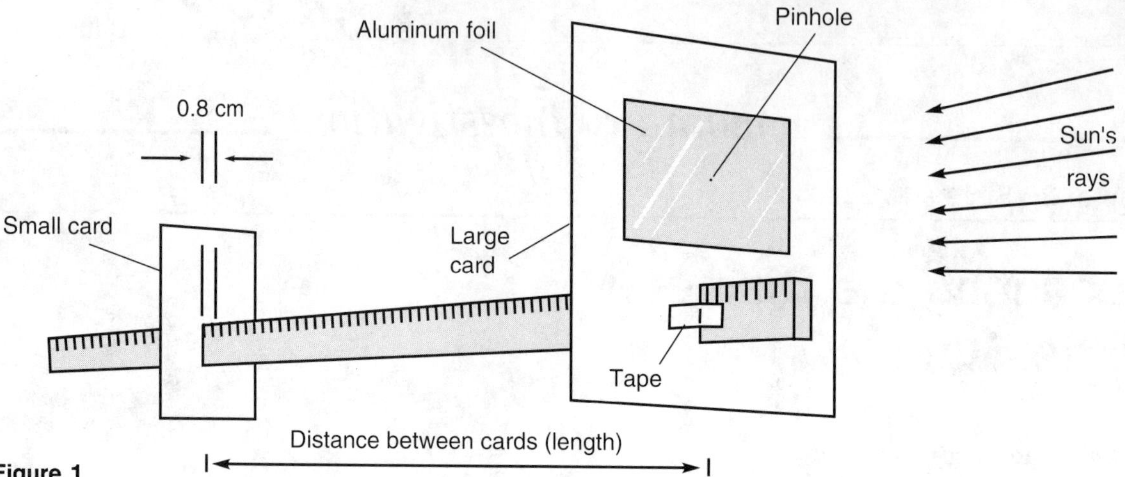

Figure 1

5. Aim the end of the meterstick that has the foil-covered card on it toward the sun. **CAUTION:** *Do not look at the sun; you may damage your eyes.* Move the meterstick around until the shadow of the large card covers the smaller card. A bright image of the sun will fall on the smaller card. Move the smaller card until the bright image of the sun exactly fills the space between the two parallel lines on the smaller card.

6. Be certain both cards are perpendicular to the meterstick. Then determine the distance between the two cards. Measure the distance to the nearest 0.1 cm and record it in the Data Table. Also record the diameter of the image.

Observations

DATA TABLE

Distance Between Two Cards	Diameter of Sun's Image

Analysis and Conclusions

1. Using the formula below, calculate the diameter of the sun.

$$\frac{\text{diameter of the sun (km)}}{\text{distance to the sun (km)}} = \frac{\text{diameter of the sun's image (cm)}}{\text{distance between two cards (cm)}}$$

Note: *The diameter of the sun's image is 0.8 cm, since it equals the width of the small card's slit.* The average distance between the Earth and sun is approximately 150,000,000 km.

2. The actual diameter of the sun is 1,391,000 km. Using the formula below, determine the amount of error in your calculated value for the sun's diameter.

$$\text{Percentage of error} = \frac{\text{difference between your value and the correct value}}{\text{correct value}} \times 100$$

______

3. What could account for your error in calculating the sun's diameter?

______

______

Critical Thinking and Application

1. How might the technique used in this investigation be useful in making other astronomical measurements? ______

______

______

______

______

2. How is the technique used in this investigation related to the construction of a camera?

______

______

______

______

3. How might clouds in the sky affect the accuracy of your measurement in this investigation? ______

______

______

______

______

Going Further

Using the value you obtained for the sun's diameter and the formula below, calculate the circumference of the sun. The value of π (pi) is approximately 3.14.

$$\text{Circumference} = \pi \times \text{diameter}$$

Using the actual diameter of the sun, which is given above, calculate the actual circumference of the sun.

Using the two values for the sun's circumference, calculate the percentage of error for the value you obtained from your experimental data.

Name ______________________ Class __________ Date ________

Laboratory Investigation

Chapter 3 The Solar System **5**

Characteristics of Elliptical Orbits

Background Information

The shape of the school track is called an ellipse. The shape of the orbit of each planet in our solar system is also an ellipse. Unlike a circle, which is a curved shape drawn around a single point, an ellipse is a curved shape that is drawn around two points. Each of these points is called a focus; together they are called the foci of the ellipse. An ellipse is described as eccentric because it is not shaped like a circle. The more unlike a circle an ellipse becomes, the more eccentric the ellipse is said to be.

In this investigation you will draw an ellipse, calculate its eccentricity, and predict the shape of the Earth's orbit.

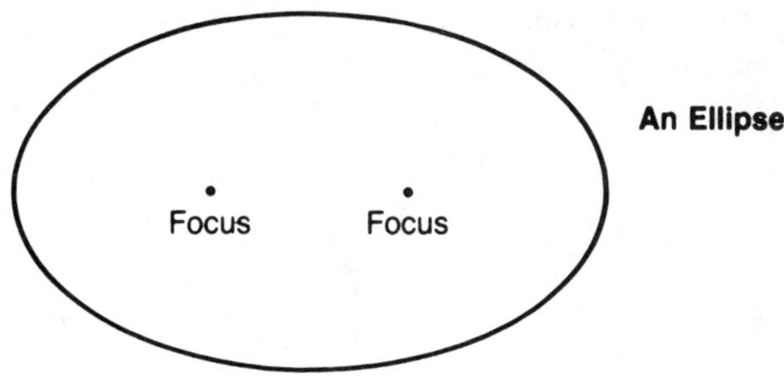

An Ellipse

Problem

What is the shape of the Earth's orbit?

Materials *(per group)*

pencil
sheet of paper
2 thumbtacks
piece of string approximately 15 cm long
piece of cardboard at least as large as the sheet of paper
metric ruler

Procedure

1. Tie the ends of the string together to form a loop.

2. Fold a sheet of paper into thirds; then flatten it out. This will help you to properly space the ellipses that you are about to draw.

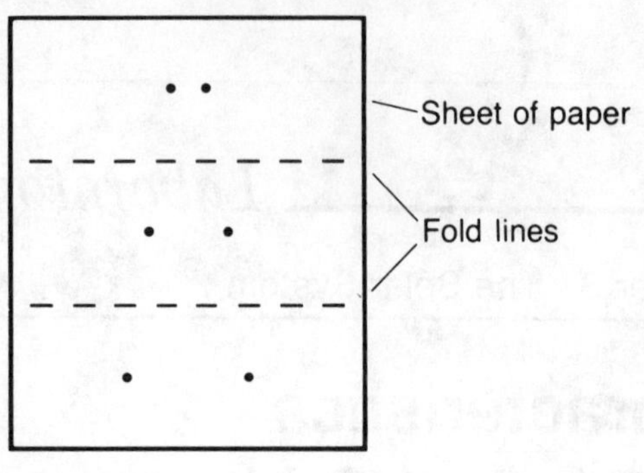

Figure 1

3. In the top third of the paper, make two dots 2 cm apart. In the middle third, make two dots 3 cm apart. In the bottom third, make two dots 4 cm apart. See Figure 1.

4. Place the sheet of paper on the piece of cardboard. Carefully push two tacks through one set of points. Place the string loop around the tacks. Then use a pencil to draw an ellipse around the two foci, pulling the string tight against the tacks. See Figure 2. Using the same procedure, draw an ellipse around each of the two remaining sets of points.

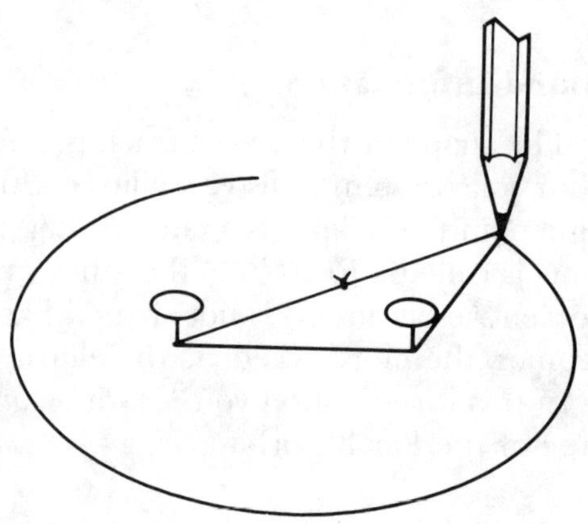

Figure 2

5. Because an ellipse is not a circle, it is said to be eccentric, or "out of round." The eccentricity, or "out-of-roundness," can be calculated and expressed as a number using the following equation:

$$\text{Eccentricity} = \frac{\text{distance between foci}}{\text{length of the major axis}}$$

Measure the distance between the foci and the length of the major axis for each of the three ellipses you have just drawn. Using the equation above, calculate their eccentricities. Enter your data in the Data Table.

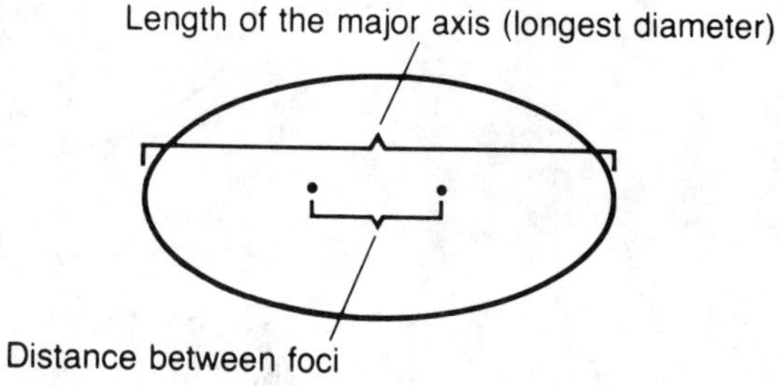

Figure 3

Observations

DATA TABLE

Ellipse	Distance Between Foci (mm)	Length of Major Axis (mm)	Eccentricity
Top (first)			
Middle (second)			
Bottom (third)			

Name ______________________ Class ____________ Date ________

Analysis and Conclusions

1. If you were drawing an ellipse, what would happen to its shape if you used the same size loop but moved the foci farther apart? ______________________

____

____

2. The eccentricity of an ellipse can be expressed as a number. Does the eccentricity of an ellipse increase, decrease, or remain the same if its shape is changed to make it more nearly round? **Note:** *Refer to the eccentricities of the ellipses you drew in this investigation.*

____

____

3. What is the relationship between the eccentricity of an ellipse and how nearly round the ellipse appears to be? ______________________

____

____

____

Critical Thinking and Application

1. The figure below represents the Earth's orbit drawn to scale. The sun is located at one of the foci; there is nothing at the other. Measure the distance between the two foci and the major axis for the orbit drawn here. Then calculate the eccentricity of the ellipse. Enter your data in the Data Table.

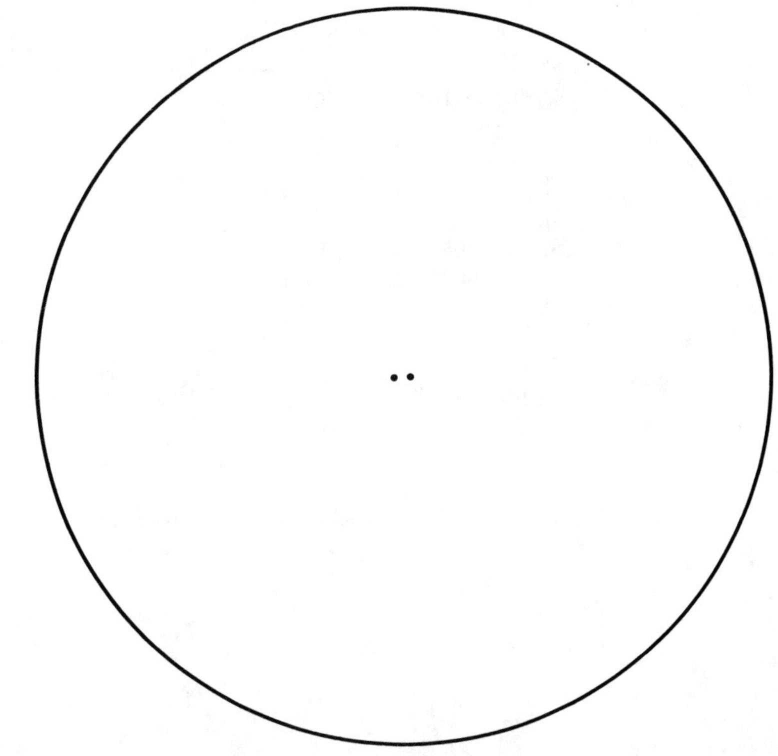

DATA TABLE

Distance between the two foci	=	____ mm
Length of major axis	=	____ mm
Eccentricity	=	____ mm

2. Does the Earth's orbit look more or less eccentric than the three ellipses you drew on the sheet of paper? ____________________

____

____

3. Which diagram most accurately shows the shape of the Earth's orbit drawn to scale?

____

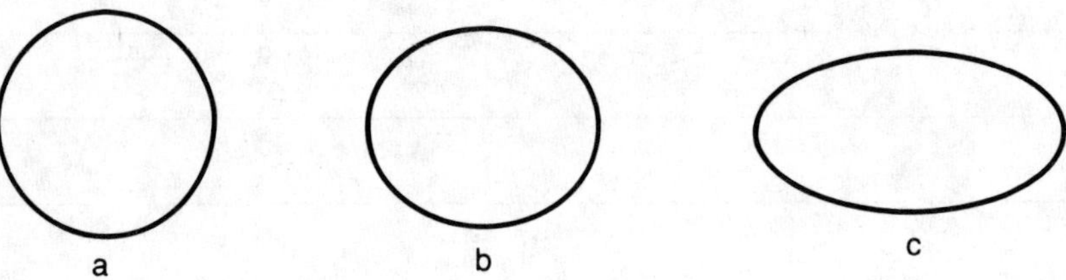

Going Further

1. Use the list of planet orbit eccentricities to answer the following questions:

Planet	Eccentricity
Mercury	0.21
Venus	0.01
Mars	0.09
Jupiter	0.05
Saturn	0.06
Uranus	0.05
Neptune	0.01
Pluto	0.25

a. Which planets have orbits that are more eccentric than the Earth's?

____

b. Which planets have orbits that are most nearly round?

____

Laboratory Investigation

Relating Gravitational Force and Orbits

Background Information

Scientists know that the nine planets in the solar system orbit the sun. They also know that the moon orbits the Earth. There is a relationship between the time it takes for a planet to orbit the sun, or its period of revolution, and the gravitational force pulling on the planet. The same relationship is also used to put an artificial satellite in orbit.

In this investigation you will determine the relationship between the period of revolution of an object or body in space and the force pulling on the orbiting object or body.

Problem

What causes planets to orbit the sun or the moon and artificial satellites to orbit the Earth?

Materials *(per group)*

15-cm glass tube, fire polished and taped
scissors
masking tape
75 cm of nylon fishing line
Styrofoam® ball, with 10-cm diameter
paper clip
25 small metal washers
metric ruler

Procedure

1. Thread a 50-cm length of nylon fishing line through the glass tube. Attach the Styrofoam ball to one end by taping the line securely. Bend the paper clip for use as a hanger. Tie the other end of the nylon fishing line to the paper clip. Your experiment setup should look like the one in Figure 1.

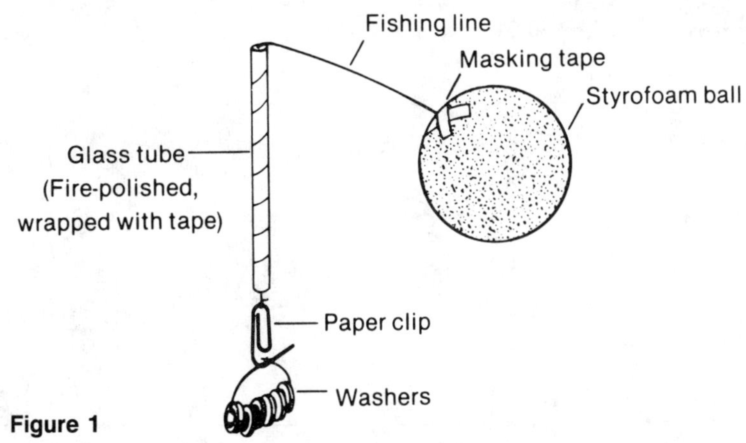

Figure 1

2. Cut a small piece of fishing line about 5 cm long. Loop the string through five washers and tie securely. Hang the loop on the paper clip. See Figure 1.

3. **CAUTION:** *Make sure that no one is near you and there is nothing for the ball to hit.* Using the tube as a handle, carefully whirl the ball around until the paper clip moves up to just below the bottom of the glass tube.

4. When the paper clip moves up just below the bottom of the glass tube, have a group member time ten complete revolutions of the ball. Find the time needed for one revolution by dividing by 10. Record your answer in the Data Table.

5. Repeat steps 2 through 4 with loops of 10, 15, 20, and 25 washers. Record each period of revolution in the Data Table.

Observations

DATA TABLE

Number of Washers	Period of Revolution
5	
10	
15	
20	
25	

Analysis and Conclusions

1. What does the number of washers represent in this model?

____

2. What happens to the period of revolution as the gravitational force increases?

____

3. Which graph best illustrates the relationship between the period of revolution and gravitational force? Explain your answer. _______________________

____

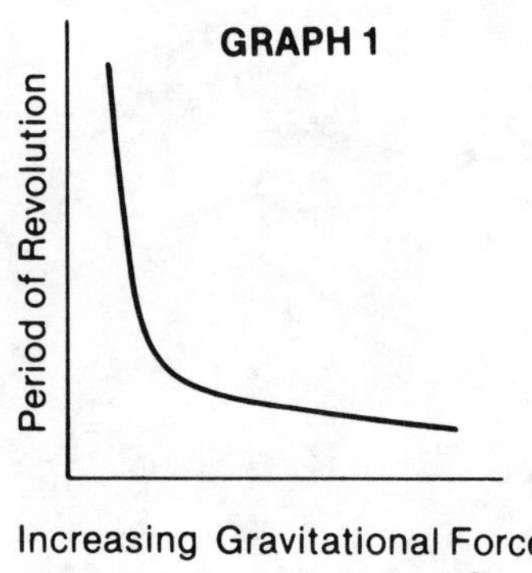

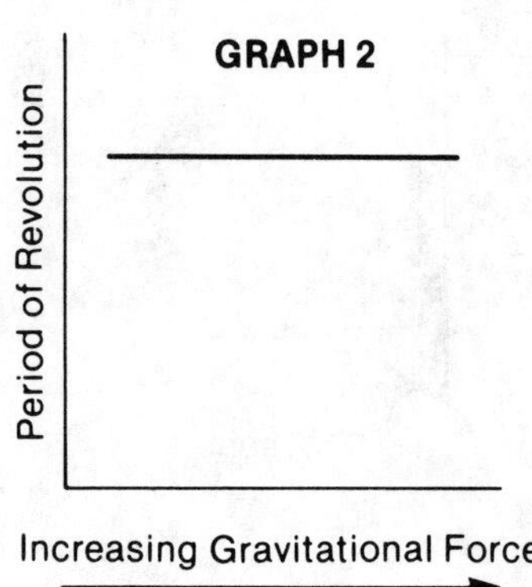

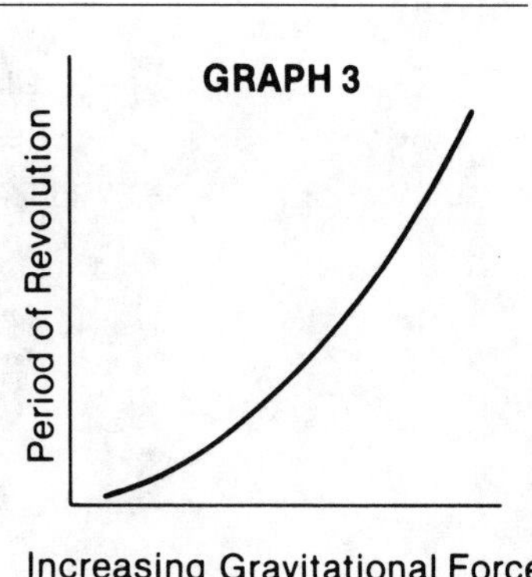

Name ______________________ Class ____________ Date ________

Critical Thinking and Application

1. Relate what you have learned in this investigation to the periods of revolution of the nine planets around the sun. ______________________

____

____

____

____

2. If an orbiting artificial satellite were to slow down, what would happen?

____

____

3. Can you think of other types of motion in which the speed of an object increases as the force exerted on it increases? ______________________

____

____

____

____

Going Further

1. Investigate how a change in mass or distance affects the period of revolution of a ball. Repeat the investigation but keep the number of washers constant and change the mass of the Styrofoam ball. How does the mass of the orbiting object affect the period of revolution?
2. Try the same experiment but change the length of the fishing line.

Laboratory Investigation

Relating Distance and Apparent Motion

Background Information

When observing an object as it moves past you, there are two factors that affect its apparent motion, or how you perceive it. The first factor is the speed of the object. Its speed is visible to you, and you call it fast or slow in relation to other reference objects. The second factor that affects the apparent motion of an object is its distance from you and from the objects around it.

In this investigation you will examine how the distance of each planet from the Earth affects its apparent movement in the sky as observed from the Earth.

Problem

How does distance affect the apparent motion of a planet in the sky?

Materials *(per group)*

tape
2 sheets of paper
scissors
meterstick

Procedure

1. Cut one sheet of paper in half lengthwise. Tape the two halves together end to end to make one long strip of paper. Tape the strip of paper to the baseboard of a wall of your classroom as shown in Figure 1. The paper represents distant space.
2. Cut out four circles from the second sheet of paper. Each circle should be 5 cm in diameter. Label the circles Planet A, Planet B, Planet C, and Planet Earth.
3. Mark a point on the right side of the paper taped to the wall. Label this point Starting point. From this point, measure 20 cm, 40 cm, 80 cm, and 100 cm in a straight line away from the wall. At 20 cm, place Planet C on the floor. At 40 cm, place Planet B on the floor. At 80 cm, place Planet A on the floor. At 100 cm, place Planet Earth on the floor.

4. Move planets A, B, and C exactly 10 cm to the left, parallel to the wall. This represents the actual motion of the planets. Leave Planet Earth in its original location.

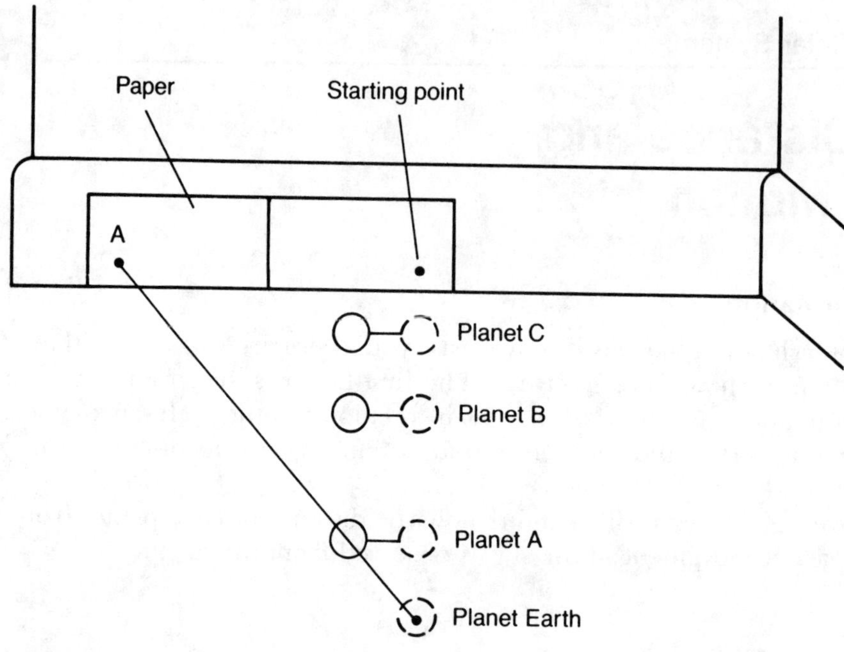

Figure 1

5. With a meterstick, mark the point on the paper taped to the wall at which a straight line running from the center of Planet Earth through the center of Planet A would meet the paper. See Figure 1. Repeat this procedure for Planets B and C. Label the appropriate points A, B, and C on the paper.

6. Measure the distances from the starting point on the paper taped to the wall to the new points marked on the paper. Write each distance on the paper next to the measured line. Record these distances in the appropriate column of the Data Table.

Observations

DATA TABLE

Planet	Actual Distance Moved	Apparent Distance Moved
A	10 cm	
B	10 cm	
C	10 cm	

Name ______________________ Class __________ Date __________

Analysis and Conclusions

1. Which planet appeared to move the farthest? ______________________

   Which planet appeared to move the least? ______________________

2. How does the apparent motion of these planets compare with their actual motion?

3. How does the distance of an observer from an object affect the apparent motion of the object as seen by the observer? ______________________

Critical Thinking and Application

1. Why do you think the apparent motion of the planets is different from their actual motion?

2. If Planet C moved twice as far during the same time, how would its motion appear relative to Planet A? ______________________

3. Why is the motion of the planets in this investigation called "apparent motion"?

____

____

____

4. Why is it important to measure the distances of the four planets straight away from the wall? ____

____

____

____

5. Why is it important to move the planets parallel to the wall?

____

____

____

Going Further

1. Explore what happens to the results of this investigation if twice the distance from the starting point (40, 80, 160, 200 cm) and twice the parallel motion (20 cm) are used.
2. Observe the motion of nearby and distant objects, such as cars, people, or airplanes. Describe how their distances from you affect their apparent motion. Which seem to move farther? Faster?

Constructing a Foucault Pendulum

Background Information

In 1851, Jean Foucault performed an experiment that was the first proof that the Earth rotates. He hung a heavy iron ball from a wire that was 61 m long. Then he set it swinging like a pendulum in a north to south line. Foucault knew that a free-swinging pendulum does not change direction. However, after about 8 hours, the pendulum was swinging in an east to west line. Therefore, the Earth rotated beneath the swinging pendulum.

In this investigation you will make a device to help you understand the principle behind Foucault's pendulum.

Problem

How can you demonstrate that the Earth rotates?

Materials *(per group)*

2 ring stands
2 burette clamps
wooden dowel about 30 cm long
thread
scissors
sheet of lined paper
fishing sinker or other small heavy object, 113 g or more in mass

Procedure

1. Set up the ring stands and wooden dowel as pictured in Figure 1. Cut an appropriate length of thread. Tie the fishing sinker to one end of the thread. Tie the other end of the thread to the center of the wooden dowel so that the sinker can swing freely like a pendulum.

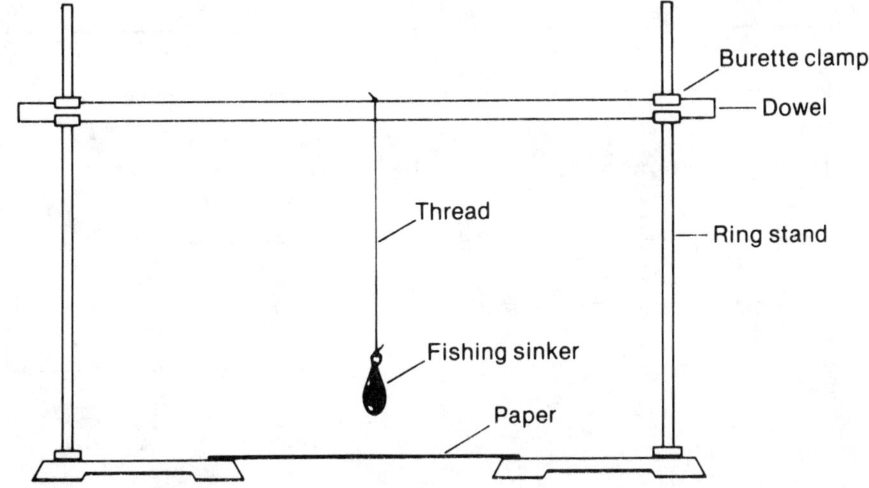

Figure 1

2. Tape a sheet of lined paper across the bases of the ring stands. The lines should be perpendicular to the direction of the dowel.
3. Several students in the group should position themselves on either side of the dowel. Another student should carefully set the pendulum swinging in the direction of the lines on the paper.
4. The students on either side of the dowel should slowly turn the whole apparatus clockwise one quarter of a full turn (90°).
5. Draw a two-headed arrow on the paper to show how the pendulum is now swinging. Label this arrow A. Observe how the direction of the pendulum has changed in relation to the students positioned on either side of the dowel.
6. The students on either side of the dowel should again slowly turn the whole apparatus clockwise another quarter of a turn (90°).
7. Draw another two-headed arrow on the paper to show how the pendulum is now swinging. Label this arrow B. Again observe how the direction of the pendulum has changed in relation to the students positioned on either side of the dowel.

Observations

1. Describe how the direction of arrow A differed from arrow B.

____

____

2. Describe how the direction of the pendulum changed in relation to the students positioned on either side of the dowel. _______________________

____

____

Analysis and Conclusions

1. If a pendulum were allowed to swing freely on the Earth, how would it appear to act if the Earth rotated? _______________________

____

____

2. How would the pendulum appear to act if the Earth did not rotate?

____

____

____

Name ______________________ Class ____________ Date ________

Critical Thinking and Application

1. Describe the changes in geographical direction that a pendulum would appear to undergo in 24 hours if it began swinging in a north to south line.

2. What happens to the swing of a pendulum, or its arc, as the pendulum is allowed to swing over a period of time? ______________________

3. What is the reason for this change? ______________________

Going Further

Construct a simple working model of Foucault's pendulum, as shown in Figure 2. Use a G-clamp with a ball bearing soldered to the inside of the jaw. Allow the ball bearing to rest on a flat, hard, and oiled metal surface. A heavy mass such as a large plastic bleach bottle filled with sand or water can then be hung from a 3-m cord. If carefully set in motion, this pendulum will appear to change direction with time. Where on the Earth would such a pendulum not change direction?

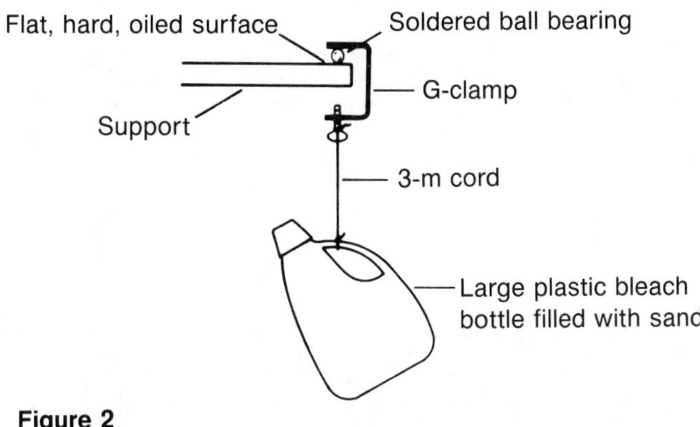

Figure 2

Comparing the Angle of Insolation and Temperature Changes

Background Information

The sun shines on each part of the Earth for the same total number of hours each year. However, there are areas of the Earth that receive more radiant energy from the sun than other areas do. Because the Earth's axis is tilted slightly and the Earth is a sphere, the sun's rays strike different areas of the Earth at different angles. The angle for a given area is called the angle of insolation.

In this investigation you will learn how the angle of the sun's rays affects temperature on the Earth.

Problem

How does the angle of insolation affect the rate of temperature change of a surface?

Materials *(per group)*

watch or clock
3 Celsius thermometers
high-wattage incandescent lamp
3 right triangular wooden blocks each with a 30°, a 60°, and a 90° angle
masking tape

Procedure

1. Using masking tape, attach one thermometer to the 30° angle of one block. Then attach the second thermometer to the 60° angle of the second block and the third to the 90° angle of the last block. See Figure 1 on the next page.
2. Place the blocks, with the thermometers attached, as shown in Figure 1. Position the lamp so that it is 20 cm from the bulb of each thermometer. This means that the blocks will be positioned along the arc of a circle having a 20-cm radius.

3. Switch on the light. Record the temperature of each thermometer every minute for 15 minutes in the Data Table.

4. After the 15-minute observation interval, switch off the light.

5. Graph your data on the graph provided. Use the key given for each of the angles.

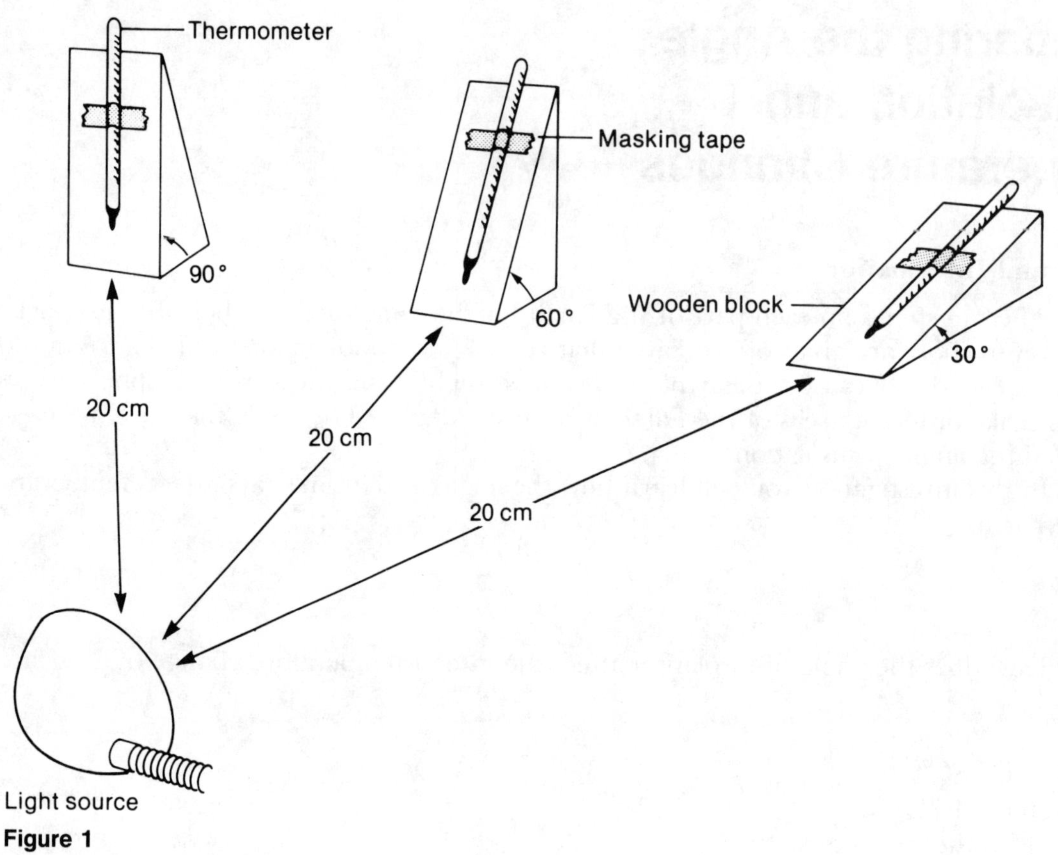

Figure 1

Observations

DATA TABLE

Angle	Time (min)	0	1	2	3	4	5	6	7	8	9	10	11	12	13	14	15
30°	Temperature																
60°	Temperature																
90°	Temperature																

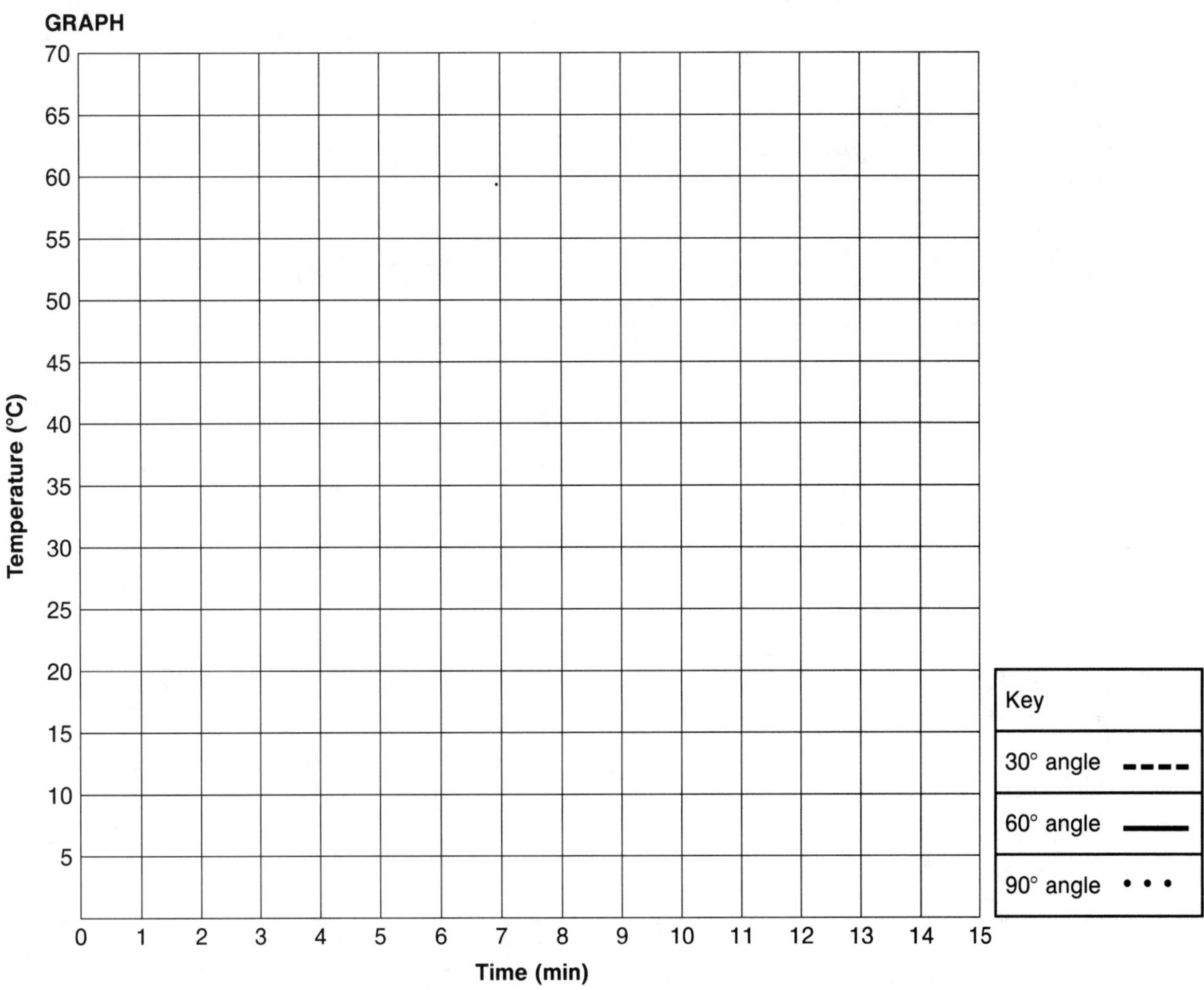

Analysis and Conclusions

1. Which angle caused the temperature to increase the most during the 15 minutes? What region of the Earth receives sunlight at this angle?

____

____

2. Which angle caused the temperature to increase the least during the 15 minutes? What region of the Earth receives sunlight at this angle?

____

____

3. What is the relationship between the size of the angle of insolation and the surface temperature? ___

___

___

Critical Thinking and Application

1. What other factors do you think influence the rate of warming of a particular spot on the Earth's surface? ___

___

___

2. Although the North Pole is tilted toward the sun in summer, its temperatures are still very cold. How can you explain this? ___

___

___

___

___

___

3. How would the results of this investigation change if the light source were placed farther from the thermometers? Closer to them? ___

___

___

___

___

___

___

Going Further

Test different soils to determine what effect soils have on the rate of heating. Prepare mounds of different types of soil. Use a protractor to be sure the angles of the mounds are the same. Place a thermometer on each mound. Keep a record of the temperature each minute for 15 minutes. Draw a graph to compare the temperature versus time for each soil.

Name ______________________ Class ____________ Date ________

Laboratory Investigation

Chapter 4 Earth and Its Moon **10**

Models of Eclipses

Background Information

As the moon and the Earth revolve around each other and the sun, they block some of the sun's light. When the sun or moon is blocked out by another object, an eclipse occurs. There are two types of eclipses—a lunar eclipse and a solar eclipse. During a lunar eclipse, the moon passes through the Earth's shadow. A solar eclipse occurs when the moon is directly between the sun and the Earth.

Shadows cast into space during an eclipse have two parts. The completely dark inner shadow is the umbra. The outer area where light is only partially blocked is called the penumbra.

In this investigation you will draw a model of a solar eclipse and of a lunar eclipse and identify the parts of a shadow.

Problem

What happens during a solar and a lunar eclipse? What are the parts of the shadows they form?

Materials *(per student)*

metric ruler
colored pencils

Procedure

1. Each step of the procedure should be done on the appropriate figure in Observations.
2. Color the sun orange, the moon blue, and the Earth green in both Figures 1 and 2.
3. On Figure 1, use the ruler to draw a line from each side of the sun to the same side of the moon. Extend these lines until they intersect with the Earth. Use the diagram below as a guide.

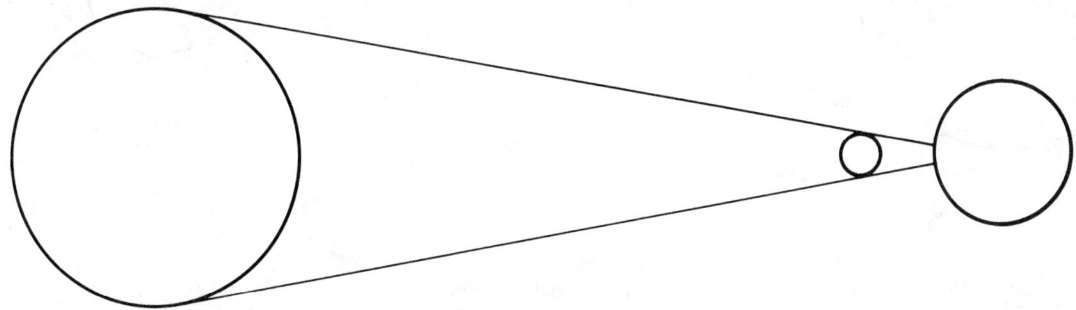

4. On the same figure, use the ruler to draw lines from the same points on the sides of the sun to the opposite sides of the moon. Extend these lines until they intersect with the Earth. Use the diagram below as a guide.

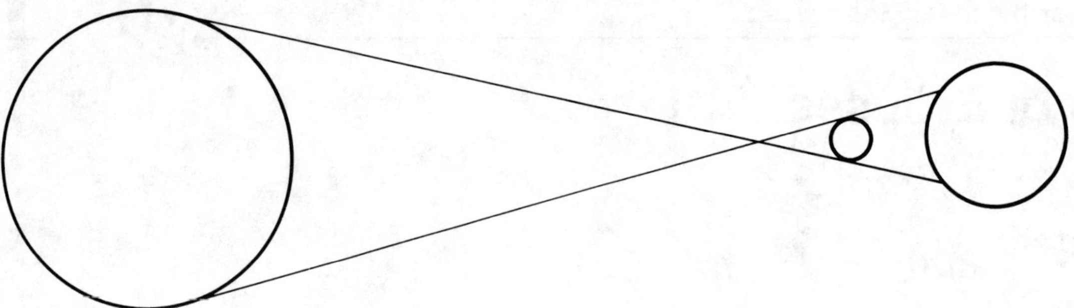

5. Color the umbra black and the penumbra purple.

6. On Figure 2, use the ruler to draw a line from each side of the sun to the same side of the Earth. Extend these lines 4 cm beyond the Earth. Use the diagram below as a guide.

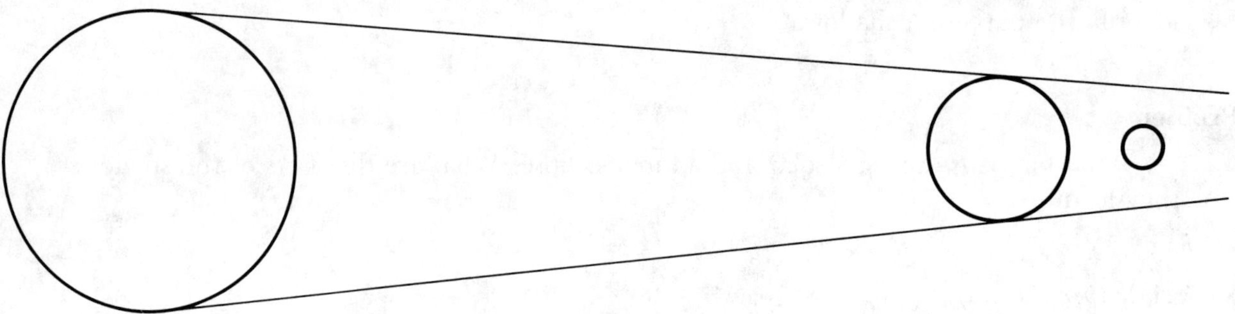

7. On the same figure, use the ruler to draw lines from the sides of the sun to the opposite sides of the Earth. Extend these lines 4 cm beyond the Earth. Use the diagram below as a guide.

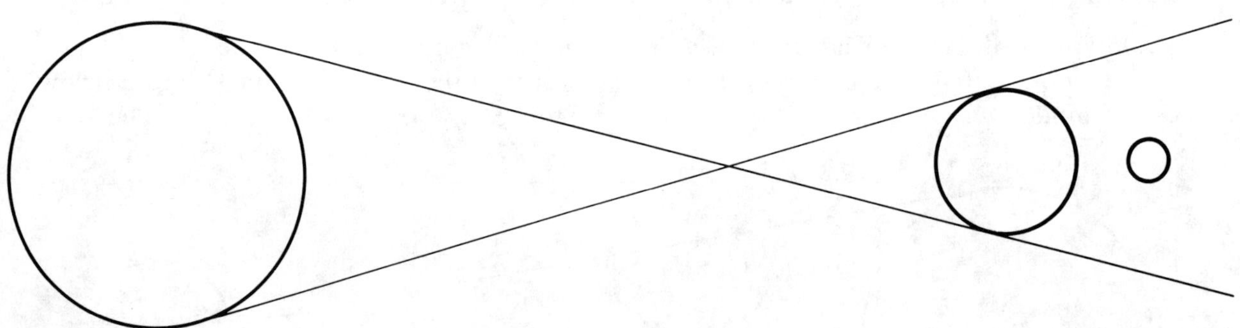

8. Color the umbra black and the penumbra purple.

Name ______________________ Class ______________ Date __________

Observations

Eclipses

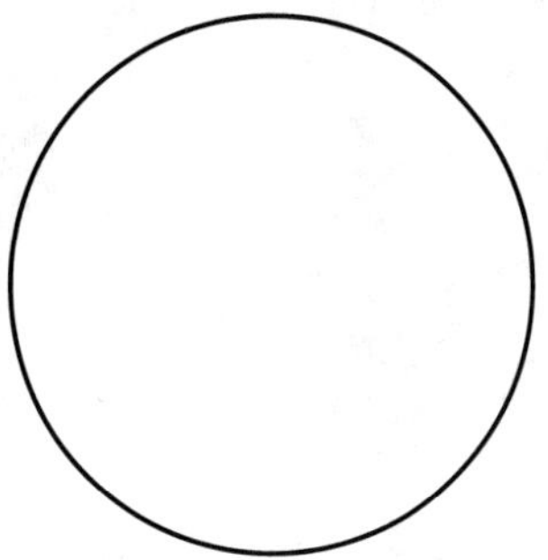

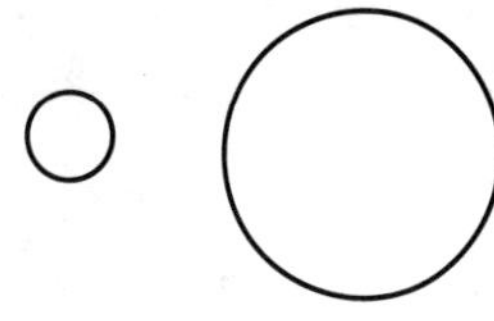

Figure 1

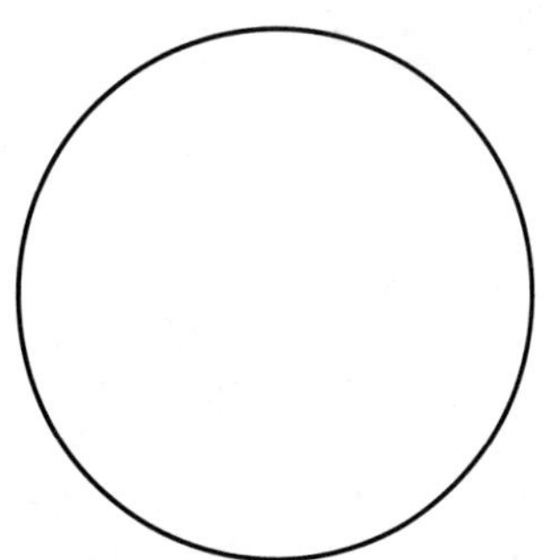

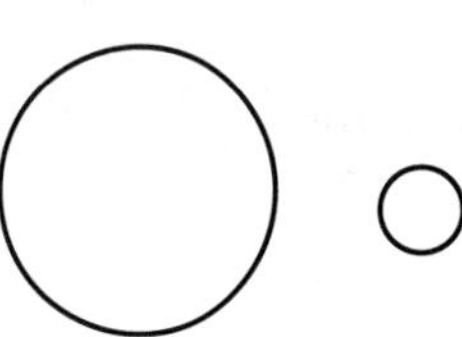

Figure 2

Analysis and Conclusions

1. What type of eclipse have you drawn in Figure 1?

   ____

   In Figure 2? ____

2. At what phase is the moon in Figure 1? ______________________________

   In Figure 2? ____

3. Which type of eclipse occurs with the greatest frequency?

   ____

4. Explain why a total solar eclipse or total lunar eclipse does not occur at least once a month. ______________________________

____

____

____

Critical Thinking and Application

1. a. If you were a lunar inhabitant, what kind(s) of eclipse(s) might you expect to see?

   ____

   b. Include a diagram to illustrate your answer.

2. Name the planets that could experience eclipses of the sun.

____

____

3. Why does our moon, which is much smaller than our sun, produce a total eclipse of the sun? ______________________________

____

____

____

Going Further

Using a light source and balls of different sizes, construct models of solar and lunar eclipses.

Name ______________________ Class __________ Date __________

Laboratory Investigation

Chapter 5 Earth's Atmosphere **11**

Finding the Percentage of Oxygen in the Atmosphere

Background Information

The atmosphere of the Earth is composed of a mixture of gases. The two most abundant gases are nitrogen and oxygen. Oxygen also appears in the Earth's crust combined with other elements to form minerals.

In this investigation you will study how much of the air is consumed during combustion. By measuring volume, you will be able to determine the percentage of oxygen in the air.

Problem

What percentage of the Earth's atmosphere is oxygen?

Materials *(per group)*

birthday candle
250-mL beaker
100-mL graduated cylinder
matches
glass-marking pencil
large test tube
penny
water
safety goggles

Procedure

1. Light the candle and let a few drops of wax drop on the penny. Blow out the candle, and place the candle upright on the penny in the wax. The candle should stick to the penny.
2. Fill the test tube with water. Using the graduated cylinder, measure this volume of water and record it in the Data Table. The volume is also the volume of air in the test tube.
3. Pour the water into the beaker. Carefully place the penny and the candle in the center of the beaker. The penny should keep the candle upright.
4. Carefully light the candle, and rapidly invert the test tube over the lighted candle. Make sure that the open end of the test tube is well under the surface of the water but not touching the bottom of the beaker. See Figure 1.

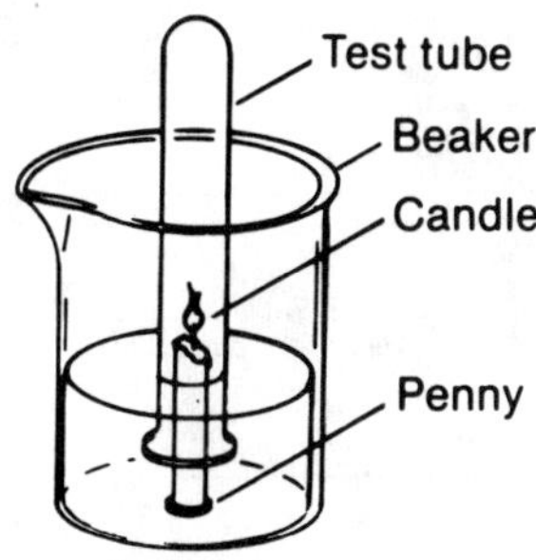

Figure 1

5. As the candle uses the oxygen in the test tube, the candle will go out and water will be drawn into the tube to replace the oxygen.
6. When the candle goes out, carefully mark the level of the water in the test tube with the glass-marking pencil. Remove the test tube.
7. Fill the test tube with water to this line. Using the graduated cylinder, measure this volume of water and record it in the Data Table. The volume is the volume of air in the test tube minus the oxygen that the candle used.
8. To find the volume of oxygen originally in the test tube, subtract the volume of air after the candle goes out from the original volume. Record the volume in the Data Table.
9. Determine the percentage of oxygen in air by using the formula below. Record this percentage in the Data Table.

$$\% \text{ Oxygen in air} = \frac{\text{Volume of oxygen in test tube}}{\text{Total volume of air in test tube at start}} \times 100$$

Observations

DATA TABLE

Volume of air in the test tube at start	mL
Volume of air in test tube after candle goes out	mL
Volume of oxygen	mL
Percentage of oxygen in air	

Analysis and Conclusions

1. Would the same result for the percentage of oxygen in air be obtained if a larger test tube was used? A larger candle? ____________________

   ____

2. Why does the water rise in the test tube as the candle goes out?

   ____

   ____

3. Nitrogen is the other major component of air (78.1 percent). What property of nitrogen have you discovered as a result of this experiment? ____________________

   ____

4. How much oxygen is present in 5 L of air? ____________________

   ____

Name ______________________ Class ______________ Date __________

Critical Thinking and Application

1. Why is oxygen such an important part of the Earth's atmosphere?

____

____

____

2. Based on your observations, what is an effective method of putting out a small fire?

____

____

3. "As the altitude of an area increases, the density of the atmosphere decreases." How can this statement be used to explain why it is more difficult to breathe in Denver, which has an altitude of more than 1500 m, than in Houston, which is at sea level?

____

____

____

Going Further

Try the same investigation with steel wool. Place a small amount of fine, moist steel wool in the closed end of the tube. Using a test-tube clamp on a ring stand, suspend the test tube upside down in a beaker of water. Let it remain this way for a few days. After a few days, note any changes. Mark any changes in the height of water in the test tube. Find the percentage of oxygen in the air. What percentage of oxygen in the air do you get using this method?

Laboratory Investigation

Effect of the Atmosphere on Cooling Rates of the Earth's Surface

Background Information

As sunlight reaches the Earth's surface during the day, it tends to heat the surface. As soon as the sun has set, ground surfaces quickly begin to cool off. Scientists have observed that temperature, motion, and other characteristics of the atmosphere in a given area are important factors that help to determine the rate at which Earth surfaces lose their heat energy. In fact, on the moon, where there is practically no atmosphere at all, heating and cooling of the ground surfaces occur at noticeably different rates than on the Earth, where an atmosphere does exist.

In this investigation you will use a model to study the rate of surface cooling due to the presence of an atmosphere.

Problem

How does the presence of an atmosphere affect the rate at which heated Earth surfaces cool?

Materials *(per group)*

2 containers holding equal amounts of dry soil
2 Celsius thermometers
1 transparent plastic covering
heat source such as a lamp
clock or timer

Procedure

1. Place the same amount of dry soil in each container. Fill the containers to within 1 to 2 cm from the top.
2. Place a thermometer in the soil of each container and adjust the thermometers so that the bulbs are just below the surface.
3. Place both containers under a heat lamp, turn it on, and allow it to remain on for exactly 10 minutes. The temperature of the soil at the end of the 10-minute heating period should be approximately 15–20°C higher than room temperature.
4. At the end of the 10-minute heating cycle, turn off the lamp, remove it, and immediately place the transparent plastic cover over one of the containers. Leave the second container uncovered.

5. Record the starting temperature at time zero (0), the time at which you turned the lamp off. Then record the temperature of the soil in each container every minute for 15 minutes. Enter your data in the Data Table.

6. Graph the data for both containers on the grid provided. Plot a separate line for each container. Identify the data by correctly labeling each curve.

Observations

DATA TABLE

Time (min)	0	1	2	3	4	5	6	7	8	9	10	11	12	13	14	15
Temperature uncovered (°C)																
Temperature covered (°C)																

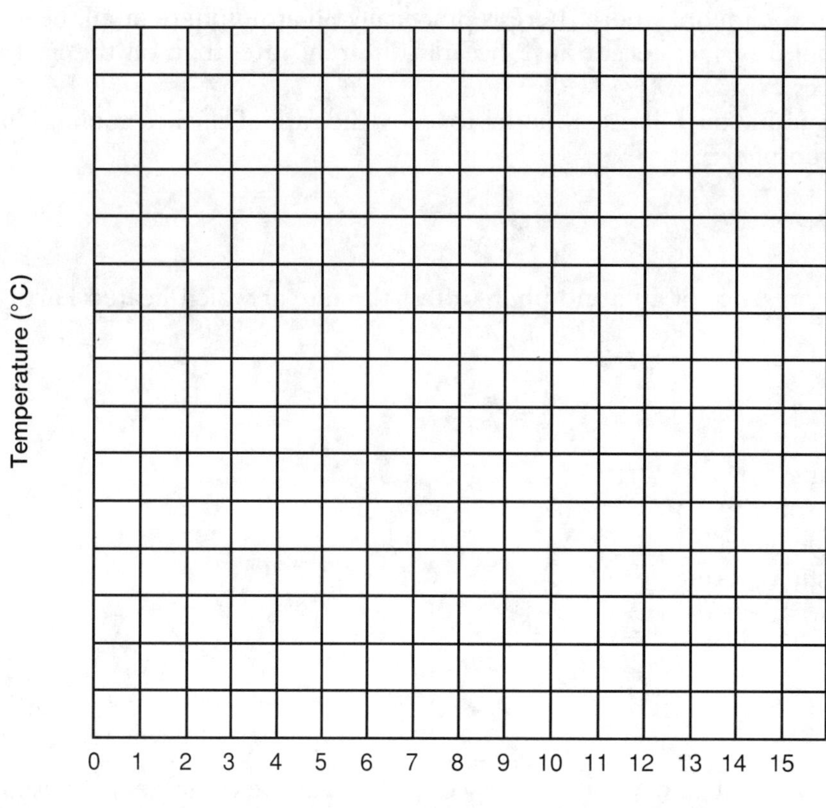

Analysis and Conclusions

1. Which container of soil received the most energy from the heat source?

____

2. In which container of soil did the temperature change the least during the 15-minute cooling period? ______________________

3. Explain why you think the temperature in that container changed the least.

Critical Thinking and Application

1. How is your model similar to the real Earth and its atmosphere?

2. How is your model different from the real Earth and its atmosphere?

3. a. What might have happened if you had used a nontransparent cover rather than the transparent one? ______________________

   b. What might have happened if you had used a transparent cover with many small holes or openings? ______________________

4. Why do you think the very coldest nights often seem to occur when there are no clouds in the sky? ____________________

____

____

____

Going Further

Design an investigation to test the hypotheses you made in question 3 of Critical Thinking and Application. Include problem, hypothesis, materials, procedure, observations, and conclusions. Identify the experimental setup, control setup, and variable. With your teacher's permission, perform the investigation. How do your observations compare with your hypotheses?

Name ______________________ Class __________ Date ________

Laboratory Investigation

Chapter 6 Earth's Oceans **13**

Relating Salinity and Density

Background Information

Scientists use a device known as a hydrometer to determine density of liquids. Using the density of a solution, you can determine the amount of material dissolved in a liquid, or the concentration. You can also determine if any more solid can be dissolved.

Salt is present in all of the Earth's oceans. The amount of salt in the ocean is called salinity.

In this investigation you will make a hydrometer and perform an experiment to determine the relationship of the density of water to the amount of salt dissolved in the water. You will add increasing amounts of salt to water and plot on a graph the water level of the hydrometer.

Problem

Does the density of water change when increasing amounts of salt are dissolved in the water?

Materials *(per group)*

2-L milk carton	waterproof marking pen	1 L of water
soda straw	metric ruler	50 g of salt
masking tape	modeling clay	triple-beam balance

Procedure

1. Obtain a 10-cm strip of masking tape. Starting at one end of the tape, draw a straight line that is 8 cm long on the tape. Using the metric ruler and pen, mark off each millimeter, making an extra long mark at each 5-mm interval. Label the marks 0, 5, 10, 15, and so on. You should now have a millimeter scale from 0 to 80.
2. Carefully place the tape scale on one end of the straw, making sure the 0-mm mark is at the top of the straw.
3. To the other end of the straw, add a small ball of clay making a watertight seal. You now have a soda-straw float. This is a simple type of hydrometer. The principle of your hydrometer is that the higher the straw floats, the greater the density of the liquid.
4. Fill a 2-L milk carton with 1 L of water. Place the soda-straw float in the water. The soda straw should float in an upright position. In the Data Table, record where the water level comes on your millimeter scale.
5. Remove the soda-straw float and thoroughly mix 10 g of salt in the water. Replace the soda-straw float and record the water level on your scale in the Data Table.
6. Repeat step 5 four more times, each time adding 10 more grams of salt to the water. Record the water level each time in the Data Table.
7. Using the data you collected, plot the information on the Graph provided.

Observations

DATA TABLE

Amount of salt	0 g	10 g	20 g	30 g	40 g	50 g
Hydrometer readings						

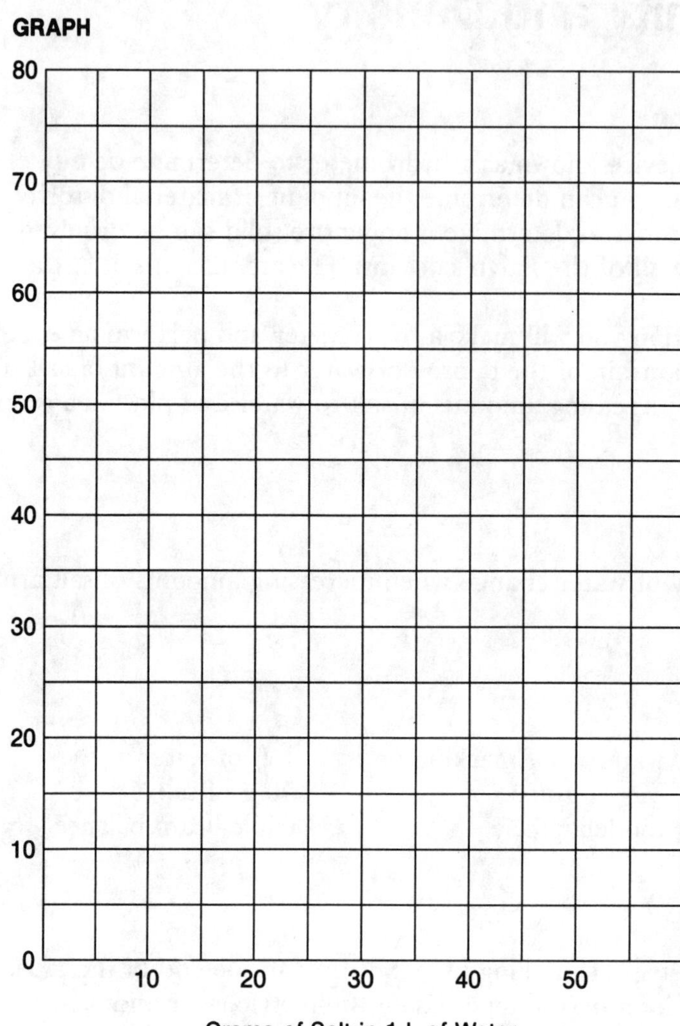

Analysis and Conclusions

1. How does a hydrometer work? ______________________________

____

____

2. As the salinity increases, does the hydrometer float higher or lower in the water? What can you conclude about the relationship of the density of water and the amount of salt added?

____

____

3. Why is it easier for a person to float in salt water than in fresh water?

____

____

Critical Thinking and Application

1. Would a boat be in more danger of sinking in the ocean or in a freshwater lake? Explain your answer. ______________________________

____

____

____

2. Why is a balloon filled with helium able to float up into the air?

____

____

3. You are given two photographs, each showing a boat floating in water. The boats in the photographs are identical, but one is floating in fresh water and the other is floating in sea water. Without being told, how might you determine which photograph is of a boat in fresh water and which is of a boat at sea? ____________________

____

____

____

Going Further

1. If you live near the ocean, obtain a sample of ocean water. Use your hydrometer to test the sample. Predict the amount of salt in grams in 1 L of the ocean water sample. Then evaporate the water and find the mass of the salt. Was your prediction accurate?
2. Design an investigation to determine if salt water freezes at the same temperature as fresh water. Include problem, hypothesis, materials, procedure, observations, and conclusions. Identify the experimental setup, control setup, and variable. With your teacher's permission, perform the investigation.

Culturing and Observing Brine Shrimp

Background Information

Brine shrimp *(Artemia salina)* are small crustaceans, a type of animal with jointed legs and a hard outer skeleton. These tiny crustaceans are often used as food for organisms kept in home aquariums. The natural environment of brine shrimp is salt water. Dried brine shrimp eggs can be stored for years if kept in a cool place. When the dried eggs are placed in saltwater solutions, they will hatch in a few days.

In this investigation you will culture brine shrimp and then examine them with a homemade water drop microscope.

Problem

What do brine shrimp look like? How do they behave? What is a water drop microscope and how does it work?

Materials *(per group)*

- 10 g of noniodized table salt or sea salt
- 2 1-L wide-mouthed jars
- graduated cylinder
- fresh water
- Celsius thermometer
- medicine dropper
- scissors or tin snips
- empty soup can
- metric ruler
- small block of wood
- gum eraser
- hammer
- no. 6 or no. 8 finishing nail
- metal file
- pocket mirror
- glass window pane
- several books
- flashlight or lamp
- sharpened pencil
- small jar
- few grains of sand, sugar, or salt
- 5 to 10 mL of brine shrimp eggs

Procedure

Part A Culturing Brine Shrimp

1. To prepare a 1 percent salt solution, add 10 g of noniodized table salt to one of the wide-mouthed jars. With the graduated cylinder, add 990 mL of fresh water to the jar.
2. Carefully mix the salt solution and allow it to reach room temperature, which is about 21°C.
3. Using the graduated cylinder, transfer 500 mL of the salt solution to the other wide-mouthed jar.

4. Measure out about 3 mL of brine shrimp eggs. Sprinkle them evenly over the surface of the salt solution in the second wide-mouthed jar.

5. Set the jar aside in an area of the classroom where it will not be disturbed. Allow the jar to remain there for two or three days.

Part B Constructing a Water Drop Microscope

1. Using the scissors or tin snips, remove the ends of the soup can. **CAUTION:** *Be very careful when cutting the soup can. It has many sharp edges.*

2. Carefully cut through the can lengthwise to form two or three strips of metal. See Figure 1. Each strip should be about 3 cm wide and 12 cm long.

3. With the scissors or tin snips, carefully snip off the sharp corners of each strip of metal. See Figure 1d.

4. Place the center of one metal strip over a small block of wood. The wood block will protect your working surface when hammering. With the hammer, carefully drive the finishing nail through the center of the metal strip.

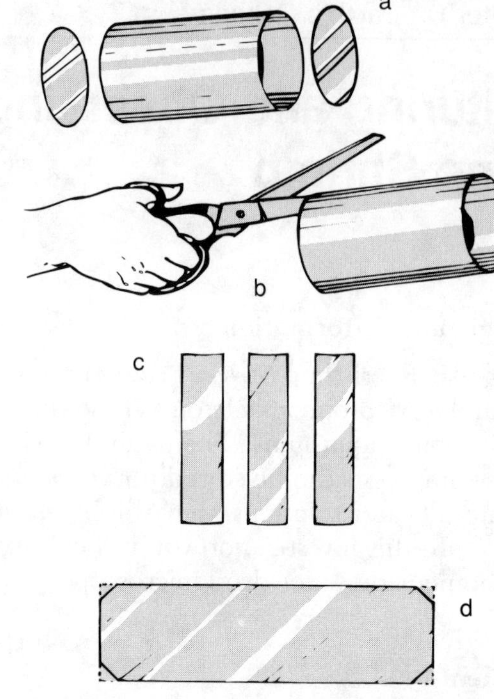

Figure 1

5. Remove the nail from the metal strip and turn the strip over. With the metal file, file down the ragged areas of the metal.

6. To make sure that the hole is perfectly round, insert the nail into the hole of the strip again. If the hole is not round, repeat steps 4 and 5.

7. Repeat steps 4 to 6 for the other metal strips.

8. Carefully bend down the ends of each metal strip slightly. See Figure 2a.

9. Now place the mirror so that it is resting against the gum eraser as shown in Figure 2b.

10. Place two stacks of books of equal height on a desk or table. Carefully place the glass window pane over the stacks of books.

11. Place the slanting mirror under the glass pane and one of the metal strips directly above it. See Figure 3.

12. Place the flashlight or lamp in front of the mirror so that the light is reflected upward through the glass pane. **CAUTION:** *Do not use reflected sunlight as a light source.*

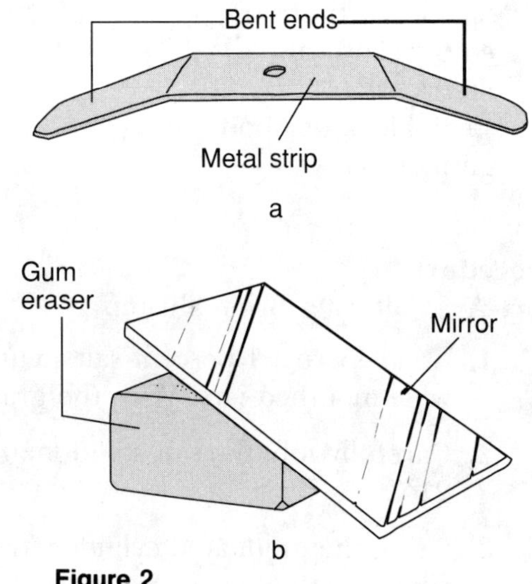

Figure 2

Name ______________________ Class ____________ Date ________

Figure 3

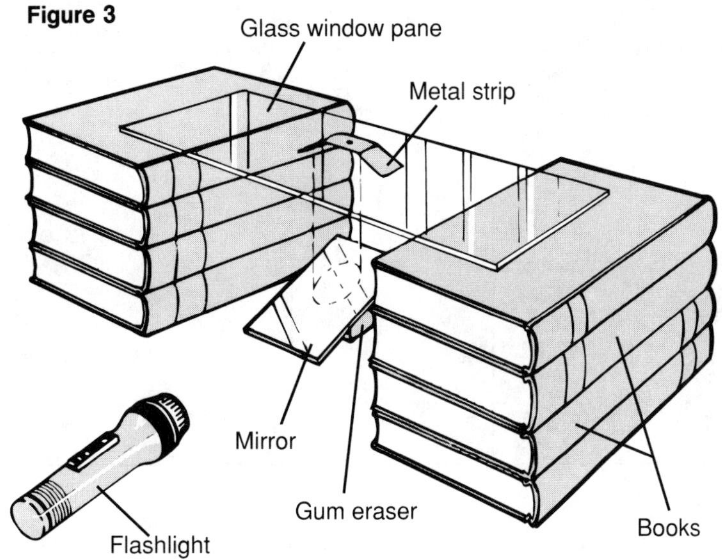

Part C Observing Brine Shrimp

1. Dip the sharpened pencil into the small jar of water. Place the pencil's point in the hole of one of the metal strips so that a fairly large drop of water is deposited over the hole. See Figure 4.

Figure 4

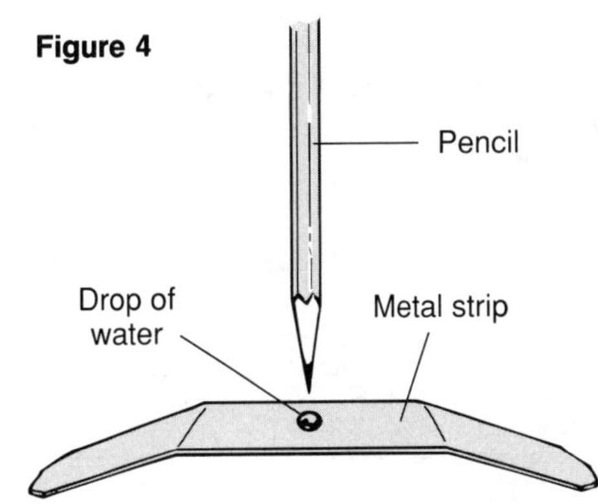

2. Sprinkle a few grains of sand, sugar, or salt on the glass pane. These materials will be your practice materials. Spread the grains evenly so that they will not be bunched together.
3. Carefully slide the metal strip containing the water drop into position directly over the material to be observed.
4. Look through the water drop. With one finger, gently press down on the metal strip until the object comes into focus. **Note:** *Do not allow the water drop to touch the objects on the glass pane.*
5. After you have mastered the viewing technique, remove the practice material from the glass pane.
6. Carefully place a few brine shrimp eggs on the glass pane. Observe the size and shape of several eggs. Notice any surface detail.
7. Wait until you see that some of the eggs in the salt solution have hatched. With a medicine dropper, transfer a few of them to the surface of the glass pane.
8. Observe the appearance and behavior of the live brine shrimp.

Observations

1. In the space below, sketch some brine shrimp eggs and live brine shrimp.

Brine Shrimp Eggs

Live Brine Shrimp

2. Briefly describe each of the following live brine shrimp characteristics.

a. Body shape and color ______

b. Distinctive markings ______

c. Number of "arms" or "legs" ______

d. Movement ______

e. Internal structure ______

3. In hours, how long did it take for most of the eggs to hatch?

______

4. a. How long did the brine shrimp survive on the glass pane?

______

b. How long did they survive in the salt solution?

______

Analysis and Conclusions

1. In addition to brine shrimp, what other organisms live in sea water?

______

______

______

Name ____________________ Class ____________ Date ________

2. List two reasons why brine shrimp are such good animals for studying growth and development. ____________________

3. Why is a water drop microscope better to use in the study of live brine shrimp than a regular microscope? ____________________

Critical Thinking and Application

1. Brine shrimp are described as being positively photoresponsive. This means that they tend to move toward bright light. Briefly describe a simple experiment by which you might test this statement. ____________________

2. Based on the information in question 1, where in the ocean would you expect to find brine shrimp? ____________________

3. How would knowing how an organism responds to light be important in using the ocean as a food source? ____________________

Going Further

With a glass-marking pencil, number five culture dishes from 1 to 5. Divide the remaining 500 mL of salt solution equally into each of the culture dishes. To culture dish 1, add 1 drop of vinegar, a mild acid. To culture dish 2, add 2 drops of vinegar, and so on. Into each culture dish, sprinkle a "pinch" of brine shrimp eggs. Allow enough time for the eggs in all the dishes to hatch. Observe the effects of increasing acidity on the hatching time, swimming activity, and survival time of the eggs that hatch in each dish.

Investigating Density Currents

Background Information

Scientists have discovered continental-type sediments on the ocean floor hundreds of kilometers from continental shorelines. Such sediments could not have been distributed so far from shore by normal wave action or surface ocean currents. Oceanographers have studied sea-floor currents and have found evidence that sediment originating from the land could be transported great distances across the ocean floor, apparently at high speeds, by a process that involves deep-sea density currents. Such currents, consisting of mixtures of mud, sand, and coarser particles, are believed to originate on continental shelves, move down slopes, and flow outward across the ocean floor for great distances. Oceanographers also believe that such density currents are somehow associated with the development of submarine canyons.

In this investigation you will create a model of a density current. You will use a mixture of clay and water, called a slurry, to observe some of the factors that affect the behavior of deep-sea density currents.

Problem

What effect do differences in density currents have on the rate at which a slurry moves down a slope? What effect do differences in slope have on the rate at which a density current flows?

Materials *(per group)*

slurry samples of different densities
plastic tube with stopper
ring stand with clamp
fresh water
protractor
4 test tubes
test-tube rack
glass-marking pencil
timer or stopwatch
meterstick
graph paper

Procedure

Part A Slurry Flow Versus Slurry Density

1. Set up the plastic tube and ring stand as shown in Figure 1. Then use your protractor to set the tube so that it forms a slope of 15° with the table top. See Figure 2.

2. Fill the plastic tube with fresh water to within 10 cm of the top.

3. Your teacher will now supply you with four containers of slurry, numbered 1, 2, 3, and 4. Slurry number 1 is the most dense slurry, number 4 is the least dense. Stir the contents of each container. Pour a sample of each slurry into a test tube until it is half full. With the glass-marking pencil, label each test tube with the number of the slurry it contains.

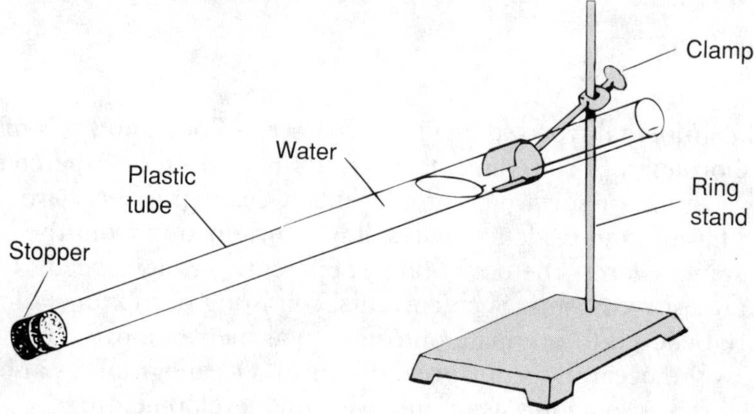

Figure 1

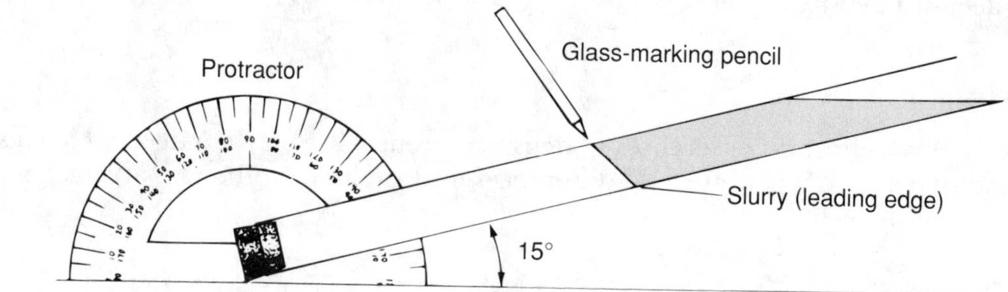

Figure 2

4. Shake the test tube containing slurry 1, which is the densest, and then quickly pour its contents into the plastic tube of water. Mark the distance the slurry travels in 5-second intervals. Use your glass-marking pencil and make your marks directly on the plastic tube.

5. Measure these distances and record them in Data Table 1.

6. Empty the contents of the plastic tube, rinse with fresh water, and repeat steps 1 through 5 with slurries numbered 2, 3, and 4.

7. Calculate the average velocity, or speed, and record your answers in Data Table 1. Average velocity is determined by dividing the total distance traveled by the time necessary to travel that distance. Prepare a graph that shows the relationship between density of a slurry and average velocity of the density current.

Part B Slurry Flow Versus Slope

1. Remove all marks from the plastic tube and refill it with fresh water. Readjust the angle of the tube so that it forms a slope of 30° with the table top.
2. Select another sample of slurry 1. Shake the test tube and again pour its contents into the plastic tube of water. Determine the total time it takes for the slurry to reach the bottom of the tube. Calculate the average velocity as you did in Part A. Record your observations in Data Table 2.
3. Empty the contents of the plastic tube, rinse it with fresh water, and adjust the angle of the tube so that it forms a slope of 45° with the table top. Repeat step 2. Then repeat this procedure with the tube set at angles of 60°, 75°, and 90° with the table top. Remember to use only slurry 1 for all angles. Record each of your observations in Data Table 2.
4. Prepare a second graph that shows the relationship between slurry velocity and slope. Your graph should illustrate flow rate for slopes of 15, 30, 45, 60, 75, and 90 degrees.

Observations

DATA TABLE 1

Slurry Density	Distance Traveled (cm) After:							Average Velocity (cm/sec)
	5 sec	10 sec	15 sec	20 sec	25 sec	30 sec	35 sec	
No. 1								
No. 2								
No. 3								
No. 4								

DATA TABLE 2

Slope (°)	Travel Time (sec)	Average Velocity (cm/sec)
15		
30		
45		
60		
75		
90		

Analysis and Conclusions

1. Based on your first graph, what is the relationship between the average velocity of a slurry and its density? ______________________________

____

____

2. a. Describe any velocity change that you may have observed in each of the slurries as they traveled down the tube. ______________________________

____

____

b. What factors do you think were responsible for any change in velocity that you observed? ______________________________

____

____

3. Based on your second graph, what is the effect of differences in slope on the velocity of slurry 1? ______________________________

____

____

Name ______________________ Class __________ Date ________

Critical Thinking and Application

1. Your investigation differed from a real density current in one very important way. A real density current moves over an ocean bottom that contains loose sediment. As a result, it stirs up these sediments and the current increases in density as it moves. Do you think your slurries increased in density as they moved down the plastic tube? What evidence would you use to support your answer? ______________________

2. If the density of a real density current increases as it continues along its path, what do you think would happen to its velocity as it travels? ______________________

3. What do you think would happen to the amount of sediment being carried as a real density current moved down a slope? ______________________

4. From your graphs and observations, do you think that density currents could be the cause of continental-type sediments being transported so far from continental shorelines? Explain your answer. ______________________

Going Further

Design an investigation that will determine the effect of temperature on the density of water. Include problem, hypothesis, materials, procedure, observations, and conclusions. Identify the experimental setup, control setup, and variable. With your teacher's permission, perform this investigation. Use your observations to draw conclusions about how this phenomenon could cause another type of density current in the ocean.

Laboratory Investigation

Investigating Porosity and Permeability

Background Information

Septic tanks are used in some areas of the United States to help filter wastewater before it goes into the groundwater system. As wastewater passes through filter materials, some of its impurities are removed. If the wastewater flows from the septic tank into the ground too quickly, there is not enough time for proper filtration to take place. The sewage may reach the surface and contaminate the water supply. If the filter materials prevented the sewage from leaving the tank, it would soon fill and back up into the residence.

Some filter materials are very porous, but not permeable. These filter materials can hold a great deal of water, but do not allow the water to pass through them. Other filter materials can hold very little liquid, but allow a lot of water to pass through rapidly.

In this investigation you will measure the rate at which groundwater filters through different materials.

Problem

What types of materials are best for filtering groundwater?

Materials *(per group)*

large juice can with the top and bottom removed
large index card
cheesecloth (30 cm × 30 cm)
pointed dowel (30 cm long)
pencils
metric ruler
masking tape
shallow pan
soil
sand
clay
gravel
scissors

Procedure

1. Place the cheesecloth across the bottom of the can and fasten it securely with masking tape.
2. Place equal layers of gravel, clay, sand, and soil in the juice can. Each layer should be about 2 cm deep. Place the gravel in first, then the clay, then the sand, and finally the soil. *Do not fill the can more than half full.*
3. Place the can, cheesecloth side down, on two pencils in the shallow pan. This setup will allow water to drain out easily from the bottom.

4. Make a hole in the center of the index card that is slightly larger than the diameter of the pointed dowel. Cover the can with the index card. Cut off a portion of the card to allow you to look in the can. Your apparatus should resemble Figure 1.

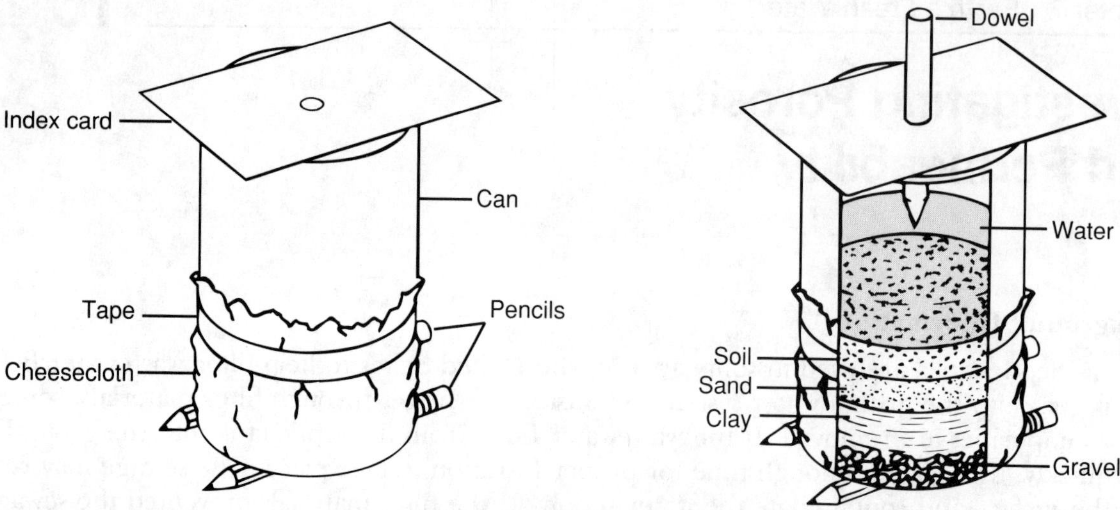

Figure 1

5. Fill the can slowly with water so the layers of material are not disturbed.
6. After 1 minute, insert the dowel until the point just touches the surface of the water. Make a mark on the dowel where it intersects the index card.
7. Repeat step 6 every minute until the stick touches the soil.
8. Determine the depth of the water in the can each minute by measuring the marks on the dowel. Record the depths in the Data Table.
9. Plot each depth against time on the Graph.

Observations

DATA TABLE

Time (min)	0	1	2	3	4	5	6	7	8	9	10
Depth (cm)											

Name ______________________ Class ____________ Date ________

GRAPH

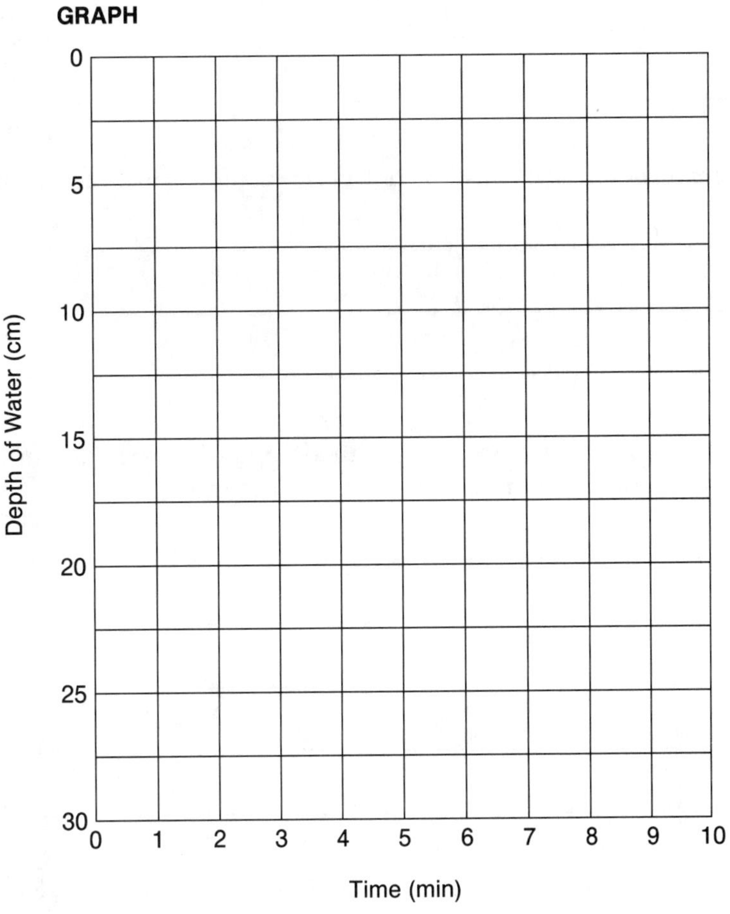

Analysis and Conclusions

1. Is the rate of filtration constant? Why or why not?

____

____

2. Which layer probably filters out impurities most efficiently? Why?

____

____

3. Which layer filters too slowly to be good for a septic tank?

____

4. Which layer would allow water to move through too rapidly to be a good filter?

____

Critical Thinking and Application

1. Why is it not a good idea to dump paint or grease into a septic tank system?

2. What common materials are porous but not permeable? Permeable but not porous?

3. If the layers in this experimental setup were made much thicker, do you think that the results of the investigation would be affected? In what way?

4. Why is it necessary to layer the materials in the following order—gravel, clay, sand, and soil?

Going Further

1. Test the filtration rates of several soils in your neighborhood or around the school. Repeat the investigation using the soils that you collect.
2. You can also test the filtration rate of sorted materials, such as sand grains, that are the same against unsorted materials, such as a mixture of gravel and sand. You also might try seeing how the filtration rate is affected if the sand and clay are mixed instead of layered.

Name ____________________ Class __________ Date __________

Laboratory Investigation

Chapter 7 Earth's Fresh Water **17**

Examining the Pollution of a Water Supply

Background Information

In many communities, water is obtained from sources deep within the ground. Groundwater very often does not exist as a pool but rather is contained in rock. Everyone must be careful not to contaminate this groundwater with pollutants.

Underground water moves in the same downward direction as surface water. The rate of movement depends on the slope of the rock layers, the kind of rock, and the amount of water. Rock layers that allow water to flow through them are called permeable.

In this investigation you will create a model of a well system and add a pollutant. You will be able to study the spread of the pollutant.

Problem

How can groundwater be contaminated?

Materials *(per group)*

1 plastic or transparent glass loaf pan
modeling clay
coarse nonsorted sand
14 heavy plastic drinking straws
red food coloring
blue food coloring
paper towels
razor blade
medicine dropper
watering can
metric ruler

Procedure

1. Cover the bottom of the pan with a layer of modeling clay. Create an incline with the clay by placing more at one end. Be sure to press the clay tightly against the bottom and sides of the pan. See Figure 1.

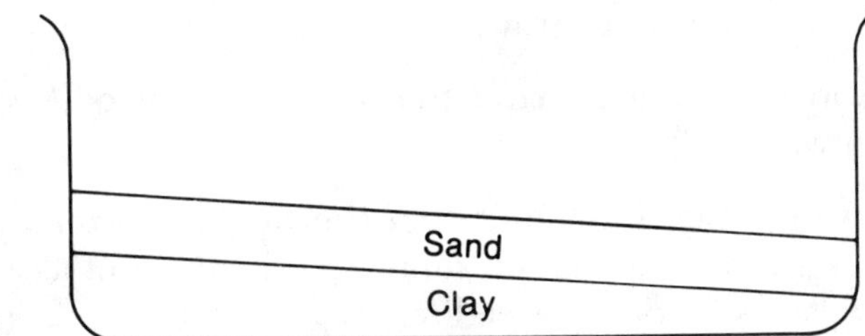

Figure 1

2. Place a layer of sand on top of the clay. The sand layer should follow the slope of the clay. Lightly sprinkle the sand with water. This is sand layer A.
3. Place a second thin layer of modeling clay on top of the sand. Be sure to follow the slope of the layers below. Press the clay tightly against the sides of the pan.

4. Finally, place a second layer of sand on top. Once again follow the slope of the layers below. Lightly sprinkle the sand with water. This is sand layer B. Your final model should resemble the model in Figure 2.

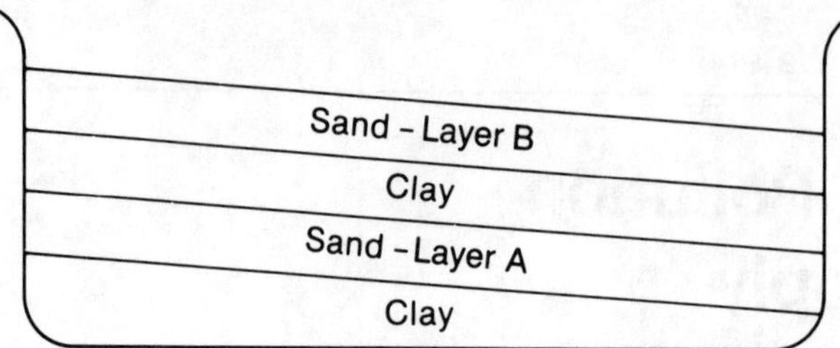

Figure 2

5. Hold your finger over the top of one drinking straw. Insert the straw into the upper end of the model about 5 cm from the highest spot on one side. See Figure 3. Insert the straw until it just goes into the bottom layer of modeling clay. Withdraw the straw. The clay and sand should come out with the straw, leaving a hole. A slight twist will help to remove the straw.

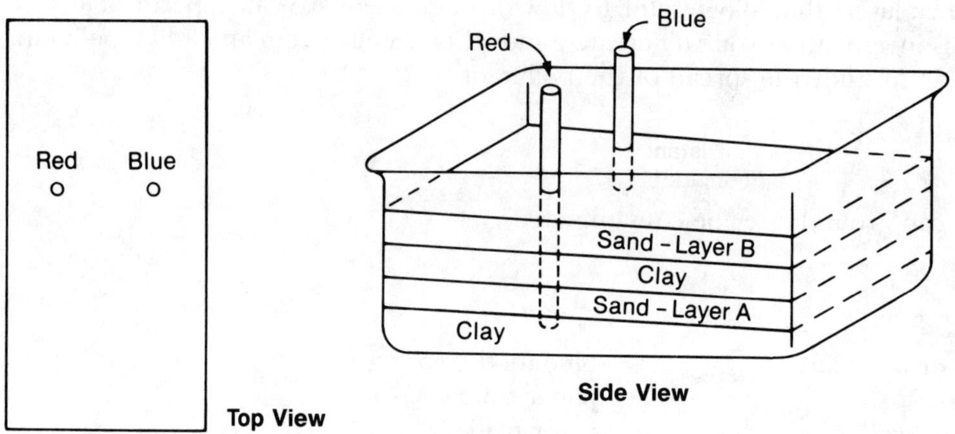

Figure 3

6. Carefully insert a new straw in the same hole to about the same depth. Using the medicine dropper, put drops of red food coloring into this straw. Remove the straw. Try not to drip the red food coloring on the surface.

7. Insert a third drinking straw as you did in step 5, but this time place it on the other half of the pan. Insert the straw into the sand only until it touches the top layer of modeling clay. Withdraw the straw. Again the clay and sand should come out with the straw.

8. Carefully insert a new straw in the same hole. Using the medicine dropper, put a few drops of blue food coloring into this straw. Remove the straw carefully.

9. The food coloring represents contaminants that have been introduced into a shallow well (blue) and a deep well (red).

10. Fill the watering can with water and lightly, but thoroughly, sprinkle the surface on both sides of the pan with water. This will simulate rainfall. Wait a few minutes for the water to soak into the layers before proceeding.

11. Take at least 10 "core samples" at various places uphill and downhill from the "wells." Do this by inserting new straws completely to the bottom of the loaf pan and removing them. For each core sample you take, record the distance uphill or downhill from the original "well." See Figure 4 on the next page.

Name ______________________ Class __________ Date __________

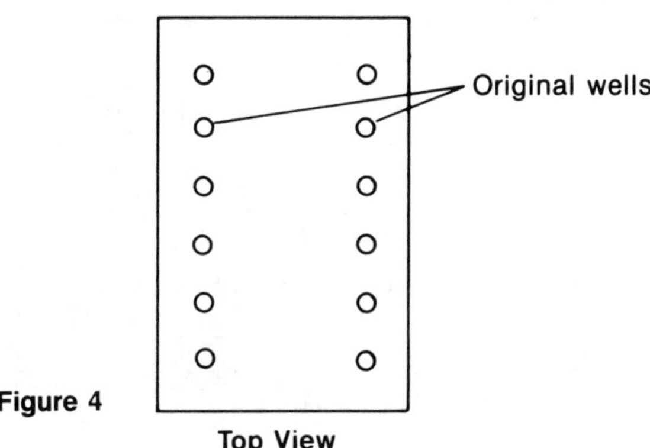

Figure 4

12. Gently lay each sample on a paper towel and carefully slit the side of the straw with the razor blade. **CAUTION:** *Use extreme care when working with a razor blade.* Examine the contents of each straw and record your observations in the Data Table. Note the presence of any color, how strong the color is, and in which sand layer it is present.

Observations

DATA TABLE

Core Sample	Distance from Wells (Indicate Uphill or Downhill)		Description of Colors	
	"Red Well"	"Blue Well"	Sand Layer A	Sand Layer B
1				
2				
3				
4				
5				
6				
7				
8				
9				
10				

Analysis and Conclusions

1. In which direction do the contaminants travel faster? Why?

____

2. In which layer do the contaminants travel faster? Why?

___

3. Did you find any red coloring in layer B? Why or why not?

___

4. Did you find any blue coloring in layer A? Why or why not?

___

5. Which layer is harder to contaminate by surface pollution? ___

6. Which layer is harder to purify if it does become contaminated? ___

7. What does the modeling clay represent? ___

Critical Thinking and Application

1. Why might toxic wastes buried in soil eventually contaminate the underground water supply? ___

___

2. How does the pollution of groundwater differ from the pollution of surface water?

___

___

___

3. Do you agree with the assertion that water in deep wells is less likely to be polluted than water in more shallow wells? Explain. ___

___

___

Going Further

Find out how hills and valleys and many different kinds of rock layers affect the movement of contaminants. Set up two models in the same way as you did in this investigation. In one model use several different types of sediment and include many layers. In another model, include hills and valleys created by folded "rock layers." Repeat the procedure in the investigation. Organize your observations in two charts. Find out if some types of sediments act as filters. Put about 100 mL of wet sand in a graduated cylinder on top of some food coloring. Invert the graduated cylinder in water. Determine if the food coloring is filtered out by the sand. Repeat the same investigation with 100 mL of gravel.

Laboratory Investigation

Chapter 8 Earth's Landmasses **18**

Constructing a Topographic Map

Background Information

All maps are models of some feature of the real world. The kind of map often used by scientists is called a contour or topographic map. Topographic maps show elevation, or height above sea level, of land areas. On a topographic map, differences in elevation are illustrated by lines that are drawn through points of equal elevation. Such lines are known as contour lines.

In this investigation you will make a contour map of a landform model.

Problem

How is a contour map created?

Materials *(per group)*

model landform in a transparent plastic box
transparent lid that fits the box
nonpermanent marking pen
source of colored water
container
blank tracing paper

Procedure

1. Check to see that your plastic box has a centimeter scale marked on one of its sides. The scale will be used to measure the level of water in the box.

2. Pour colored water into the plastic box up to the 1-cm mark. Notice that the water forms a shoreline with the landform model. See Figure 1.

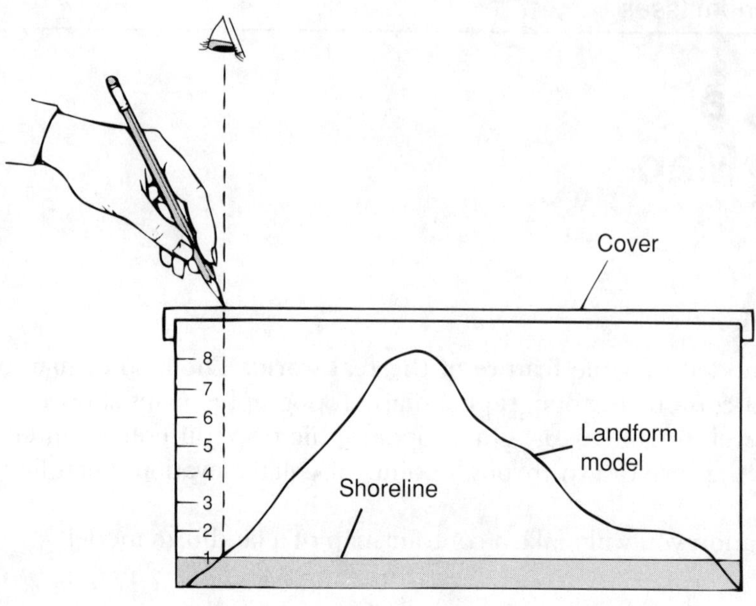

Figure 1

3. Place the cover on the box. Using the marking pen, trace the shoreline onto the cover where the colored water meets the landform model. Look straight down at the shoreline as you trace it. See Figure 1 again.

4. Continue filling the container with colored water, 1 cm at a time. Trace the new shoreline formed after each filling. When you have completely covered the landform model, you will have created a contour map of that landform. See Figure 2.

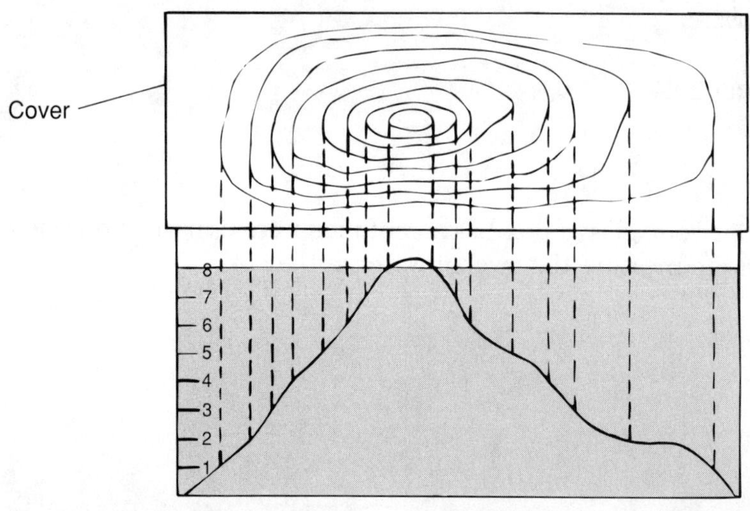

Figure 2

5. Remove the cover from the plastic box, which is now filled with colored water. Carefully pour the colored water back into the large container from which you took it. Remove a small amount at a time.

6. Place a sheet of tracing paper over the contour map that you have traced on the cover and trace the map onto the paper. You may find that if you hold the cover against a window glass, the sunlight behind it will make it easier to see the contour lines. Each student in your group should trace his or her own map from the one you made together on the lid of the box.

7. After tracing the contour lines onto your tracing paper, wash the lines from the cover. Return all materials to the proper place.

Observations

1. In this model, the vertical distance between the bottom of the box and the first horizontal line (surface of the water) is the contour interval. On a contour map, the contour interval is the vertical distance between two successive contour lines. What is the contour interval of the map you made? ______

2. Label the height of each contour line on the map that you made.

Analysis and Conclusions

1. What is the height of the highest point on the topographic map that you made?

______

______

2. According to your map, is the slope from the shoreline to the highest point on the landform uniform on all sides? How can you tell?

______

______

______

______

3. How would your topographic map be different if the landform you mapped was a large plateau? ______

______

______

______

Critical Thinking and Application

When answering the following questions, refer to the accompanying map of the island of Ert.

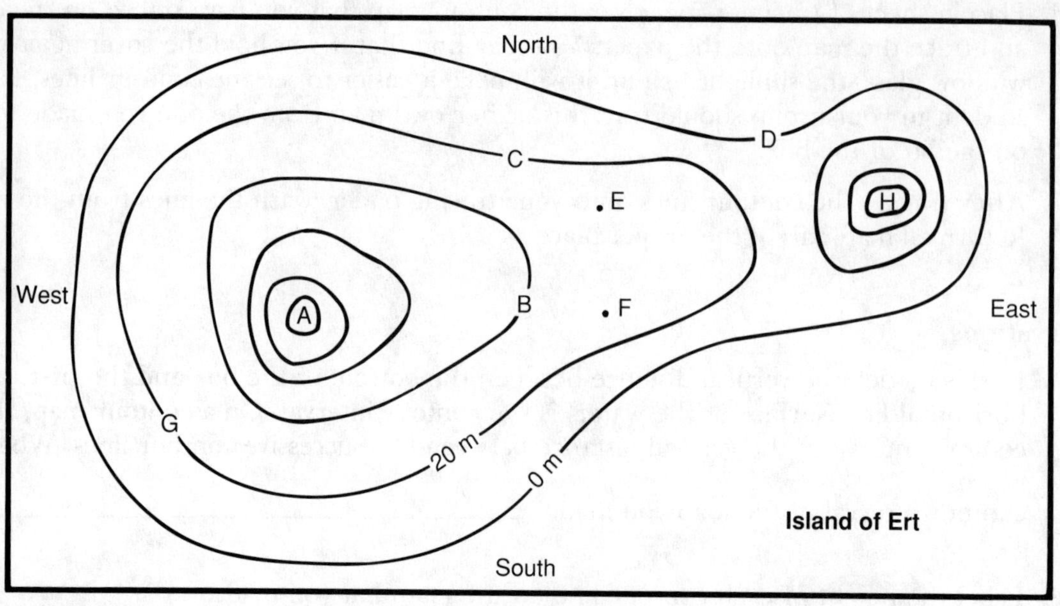

1. What is the contour interval of the map of the island of Ert?

___

2. Label the height of each contour line on the map of the island. ___

3. What two points on the map have the same elevation?

___

___

4. What is the approximate elevation of point H?

___

5. How many mountains or hills are there on the island of Ert?

___

6. Determine the approximate elevation of the highest point on the island.

___

7. If you were to walk along the 20-m contour line from point C to point G, would your elevation increase, decrease, or remain the same?

___

Going Further

Using cardboard or clay, make a three-dimensional model of the island of Ert.

Name ______________________________ Class ______________ Date __________

Laboratory Investigation

Chapter 8 Earth's Landmasses **19**

Using a Topographic Map

Background Information

When properly understood, topographic maps can be used to show the surface features of an area. Contour lines, a scale, and various symbols help to provide a realistic model of the actual geography of the area.

In this investigation you will use a simplified topographic map to locate a downed pilot.

Problem

How can topographic maps be used?

Materials *(per group)*

metric ruler
pencil

Procedure

1. Pretend that you have received the following radio message from an aircraft. "SOS . . . SOS. Come in New Hope, losing altitude, dropping . . . heading due north, altitude 3500 ft, over crossroads, now veering west, altitude now 3300 ft, ridge approaching, veering east, altitude 3200 ft . . . must land . . . ."
2. Use this information and the topographic map in Figure 1 to locate the pilot.
3. Trace the probable path taken by the pilot on the topographic map.
4. Locate the most probable area in which to conduct the search.

Observations

1. Describe the probable path taken by the pilot. ______________________________

____

____

2. What are the latitude and longitude of the most probable area in which to conduct the search? ______________________________

____

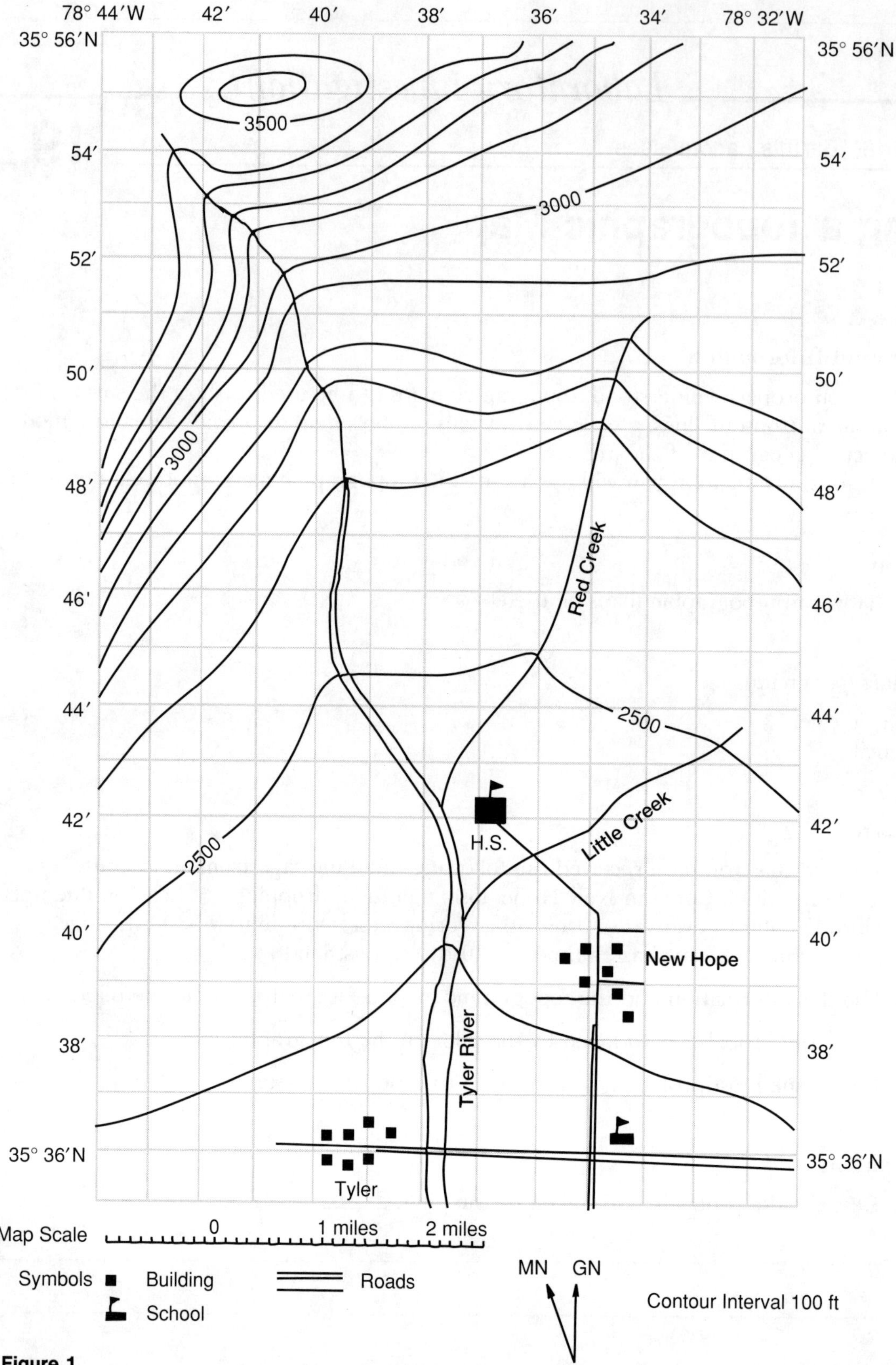

Figure 1

Analysis and Conclusions

1. Using the scale in Figure 1, how far was it from Little Creek H.S. to the location of the pilot? ______________________________

2. Locate the latitude and longitude of the highest elevation on the map.

3. In which direction does the Tyler River flow?

Critical Thinking and Application

1. What "clues" in the pilot's radio call for help make it possible to locate her?

2. Why did the pilot radio to New Hope rather than to Tyler?

3. What factor in the pilot's situation might make an emergency landing difficult?

Going Further

1. Draw a profile of one area of the map used in this investigation on graph paper across any of the latitude lines.
2. Using cardboard or clay, make a three-dimensional model of the same area. You may want to put in buildings, roads, and so on.

Laboratory Investigation

Chapter 9 Earth's Interior **20**

Observing the Action of Gases in a Magma

Background Information

Molten rock inside the Earth is called magma. Often gases are formed within the magma. These gases and some very hot liquids are less dense than the surrounding material and they rise to the surface. As they rise, some other materials may be carried with them.

In this investigation you will create an artificial magma and observe its behavior.

Problem

How can you demonstrate the action of gases in a magma?

Materials *(per group)*

600-mL beaker
6 mothballs
125 mL of baking soda
125 mL of vinegar
250 mL of water
measuring cup
glass stirring rod

Procedure

1. Mix 125 mL baking soda and 250 mL water in the 600-mL beaker until the baking soda is dissolved.
2. Place about six mothballs in the beaker and let them settle.
3. Add 125 mL of vinegar to the beaker and stir vigorously. See Figure 1.
4. Observe what happens to the mothballs.

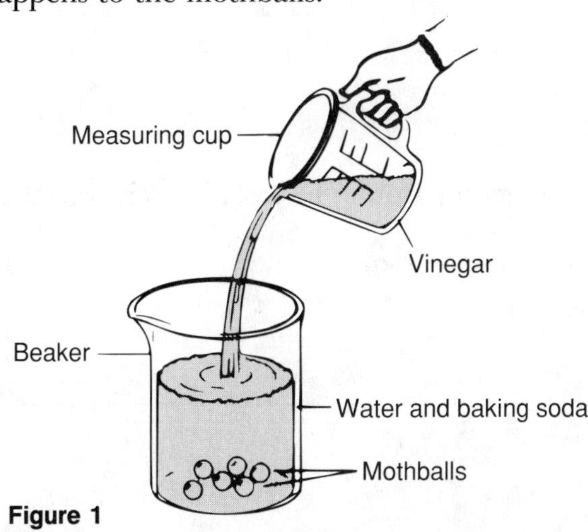

Figure 1

Observations

1. Describe the action of the mothballs after the addition of vinegar.

2. What did you notice collecting on the surface of the mothballs?

3. What do you think is happening in the beaker? Explain your answer.

Analysis and Conclusions

1. Are mothballs more or less dense than water? How do you know?

2. When the vinegar reacts with the baking soda, carbon dioxide gas is formed. What causes the action of the mothballs?

3. Why does the action of the mothballs stop after awhile?

4. Why does material rise to the surface of magma before it cools?

Critical Thinking and Application

1. Why are olivine crystals sometimes found in basaltic rock even though olivine is more dense than the basaltic lava that hardened?

2. What do you think might happen if the mass of the mothballs were greatly increased while the quantities of other ingredients in the beaker remained the same?

______

______

______

3. Convection currents in the air are formed when less dense warmer air rises above more dense cooler air. Based on this investigation, how might convection currents help reduce air pollution in a city? ______

______

______

______

Going Further

1. Explain why gold miners like to search for gold near intrusions of rock. Intrusions occur when molten rock is forced into cracks in existing rock.
2. Explain why diamonds, formed under great pressure deep in the Earth, can sometimes be found in rock close to or at the Earth's surface.

Determining the Density of the Earth

Background Information

The Earth's interior consists of four main layers: inner core, outer core, mantle, and crust. The most dense layer is the inner core; the least dense layer is the crust. The crust is made up primarily of granite, basalt, and slate. The inner and outer cores are composed mainly of iron.

In this investigation you will determine the average density of the Earth by finding the densities of the primary components of the crust and inner core.

Problem

How can the average density of the Earth be determined?

Materials *(per group)*

triple-beam balance
graduated cylinder
water
rock samples of granite, basalt, and slate
sample of iron

Procedure

1. Using the triple-beam balance, determine the mass of each rock sample. Record the measurements in the Data Table.
2. Determine the volume of each rock sample using water displacement. Record the results in the Data Table.
3. Repeat steps 1 and 2 for the iron sample.
4. Determine the density of each rock sample and of the iron sample by using the following formula:

$$\text{Density} = \frac{\text{Mass (g)}}{\text{Volume (cm}^3\text{)}}$$

Record the densities in the Data Table.

Observations

DATA TABLE

Sample	Mass (g)	Volume (cm^3)	Density (g/cm^3)
Granite			
Basalt			
Slate			
Iron			

Conclusions

1. Determine the average density of the three rock samples by adding the three densities together and dividing by 3. Record your result below.

____

2. How does the density of the iron sample compare with the average density of the rock samples? ____

____

____

3. In the space below, add the density of the iron sample to the average density of the rock samples and divide by 2. This value represents the density of the Earth. What is your experimental value for the density of the Earth?

____

4. The known density of the Earth is 5.5 g/cm^3. How does your experimental value compare with the known density? ____

____

Name ______________________ Class ____________ Date ________

Critical Thinking and Application

1. What layer of the Earth do the three rock samples represent?

____

2. What layer of the Earth does the iron sample represent?

____

3. Why is it not necessary to represent the mantle in this investigation?

____

____

____

Going Further

Find out what elements make up the mantle. Then design an investigation to determine the average density of the mantle. State your hypothesis, materials, and procedure. With your teacher's permission, perform the investigation and record your observations and conclusions.

Name ______________________ Class __________ Date __________

Laboratory Investigation

Chapter 9 Earth's Interior **22**

A Model of the Earth's Interior

Background Information

Because scientists cannot observe the internal structure of the Earth directly, they must use information from other sources to develop a model of the Earth's interior. The model of the Earth's interior developed by scientists is based on data from seismic waves. Seismic waves are vibrations that travel outward from the focus, or underground point of origin, of an earthquake. As seismic waves travel through the Earth to the surface, their speed and direction change. These changes in the speed and direction of seismic waves are due to the differences in structure and composition of the Earth's interior.

From their study of seismic waves, scientists believe that the Earth is made up of four main layers: crust, mantle, outer core, and inner core. The crust and mantle are further divided by a thin boundary called the Moho.

In this investigation you will analyze a model of the Earth's interior and relate it to what scientists believe the Earth's structure is like.

Problem

How can a classroom model of the Earth be used to illustrate the model of the Earth developed by scientists using seismic waves?

Materials *(per student)*

classroom models of the Earth's interior

Procedure

1. After selecting a model, examine its shape (external structure) for similarities and differences to the shape (external appearance) of the Earth.
2. Carefully divide the model in half.
3. Examine the model's cross section.

Observations

1. Does the model resemble the structure of the Earth? Explain.

____

____

2. Complete the chart below by listing the ways in which your classroom model is similar to and different from the model developed by scientists using seismic waves.

Similarities	Differences

3. In the circles provided, draw and label a cross-section of your classroom model and the model of the Earth developed by scientists using seismic waves.

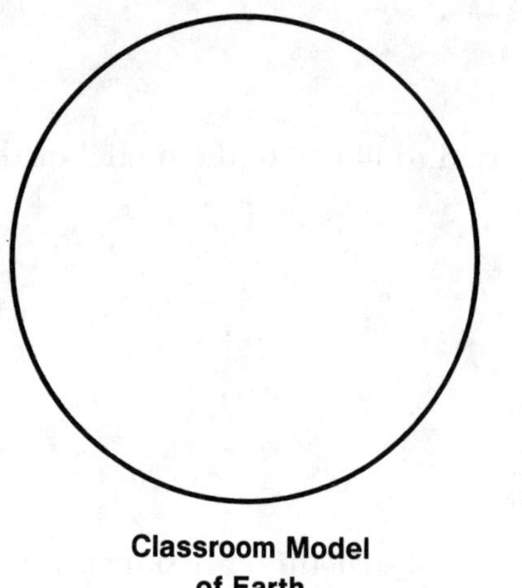

Classroom Model of Earth

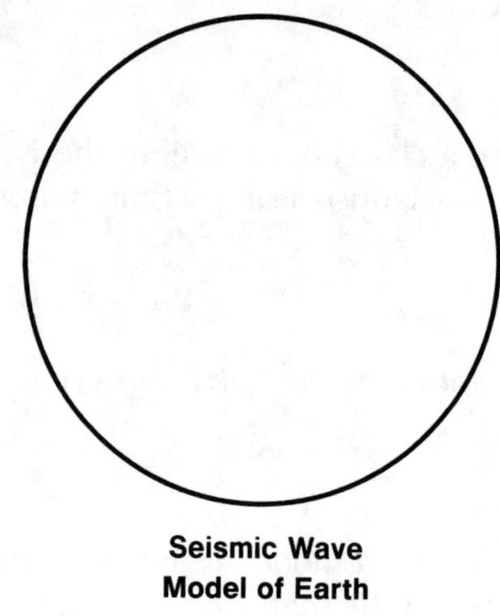

Seismic Wave Model of Earth

Analysis and Conclusions

1. What part of the model, if any, represents the crust of the Earth?

____

2. Is the Moho present in your model? _______________

____

____

3. What part of the model, if any, represents the mantle of the Earth?

____

4. What part of the model, if any, represents the outer core of the Earth?

____

____

5. What part of the model, if any, represents the inner core of the Earth?

____

Critical Thinking and Application

1. Why are models useful in the study of earth science?

____

____

2. Could scientists develop a model of the interior structure of other planets in our solar system using seismic waves? If so, how would they carry out their experiments?

____

____

____

____

____

3. a. What other earth science topics are studied using models?

____

____

____

b. Why do we have to use models to study these topics?

____

____

____

____

4. Suppose an earthquake has occurred along the San Andreas fault in Southern California. Would the seismogram recorded in Denver, Colorado be the same as the seismogram recorded in the Soviet Union? Explain your answer.

____

____

____

____

Going Further

What other items could you use as a model of the Earth's internal structure? Describe what parts of these items resemble parts of the Earth.

Name ______________________ Class __________ Date ________

Laboratory Investigation

Chapter 10 Movement of the Earth's Crust **23**

Examining Faulting and Folding

Background Information

Extremely high pressures and temperatures exist deep in the Earth. Because of these high pressures and temperatures, there is stress on the rocks. Sometimes this stress causes the rocks to bend and fold. Sometimes stress causes rocks to break and move. Breaks along which movement occurs are called faults. These folded or faulted rock layers may be exposed at the Earth's surface.

In this investigation you will examine the processes of folding and faulting.

Problem

How can clay models be used to demonstrate several types of folds and faults?

Materials *(per student)*

3 different colors of modeling clay
waxed paper
knife
golf ball

Procedure

1. Knead and flatten each of the pieces of modeling clay into thin layers on a sheet of waxed paper. Place the layers on top of each other. Using the knife, carefully cut the clay into a large rectangle. **CAUTION:** *Be very careful when using a knife.* The clay will represent the original way the rock layers were formed. Draw and label a cross section, or cut-away view, of the layers in the space provided in Observations.
2. Apply pressure with both hands at either end of the layers as shown in Figure 1.

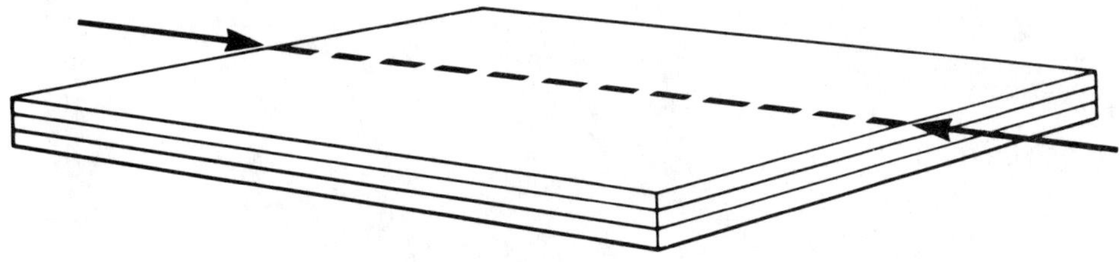

Figure 1

3. Using the knife, carefully cut a cross section through the center of the piece of clay in the same direction that you applied the pressure. See dotted line in Figure 1. Draw the cross section in the space provided in Observations.

4. Take one half of the folded layers and carefully flatten them again. Place the golf ball under the center and push the layers of clay down over it. Remove the ball. Carefully cut through the clay so that you have a cross section of the model of a dome mountain. Draw and label the cross section of the model dome mountain in the space provided in Observations.

5. Take the other half of the folded layers and carefully flatten them too. Then cut across the layers in a direction perpendicular to the original cut. **Note:** *Do not move the clay after you cut it in half.* Now apply pressure with both hands, as shown in Figure 1. You have created a fault. Draw and label a side view of the layers after movement along the fault in the space provided in Observations.

Observations

Cross Section of Unfolded Clay Layers

Cross Section of Folded Layers

Cross Section of Dome Mountain

Name ______________________ Class __________ Date ________

Cross Section of a Fault

Analysis and Conclusions

1. According to your first drawing, which rock layer would have been formed first?

   Last? ______________________

2. Using your second drawing as a reference, answer these questions.
   a. If a syncline were worn away, would you find the oldest rocks at the center or at the edge? Why? ______________________

   b. If an anticline were worn away, would you find the oldest rocks at the center or at the edge? Why? ______________________

3. How can you tell which side of a fault has risen in relation to the other side?

Critical Thinking and Application

1. How are the processes of mountain and valley formation related to faulting?

2. Why must a geologist be careful in trying to determine the ages of rock layers found in a fault or fold?

3. When a rubber band is stretched too much, it will break. How does this relate to the rock faulting?

Going Further

Using shoe boxes and crayons, prepare block diagrams of a syncline, anticline, and dome mountain. Color the layers to show the features and then label them. Construct a shoe-box block model of a fault.

Name ________________ Class ________ Date ________

Laboratory Investigation

Chapter 11 Earthquakes and Volcanoes **24**

Locating an Epicenter

Background Information

Whenever an earthquake occurs, shock waves spread out in all directions. Some of these waves cause rock particles to vibrate from side to side as they pass through the rock. Other types of waves cause rock particles to vibrate forward and backward. Different types of earthquake waves travel through rocky material at different speeds. The earthquake shock waves that travel fastest are known as P, or primary, waves. P waves are also sometimes called push-pull waves. Certain slower waves are referred to as S, or secondary, waves. S waves, also known as shear waves, are the type that cause rock particles to vibrate from side to side. S waves reach locations distant from the earthquake's point of origin somewhat later than P waves. The underground point of origin is called the earthquake's focus. The point on the land surface directly above the focus is known as the epicenter.

To detect earthquake shock waves, geologists use a very sensitive instrument called a seismograph. It can detect even the weakest of shock waves. From the information recorded by a seismograph, scientists are able to determine the exact arrival times of both P and S waves. Since P waves travel faster than S waves, you have probably realized that you can determine how far away you are from the earthquake's epicenter if you know the difference in the arrival time of the two types of waves. And that is exactly how seismologists determine the distance to an earthquake's epicenter, even when it is thousands of kilometers away. When similar information from stations in different locations is compared, the precise location of the epicenter can be determined.

In this investigation you will duplicate this procedure in a model situation.

Problem

How can an earthquake's epicenter be located?

Materials *(per student)*

drawing compass with pencil
the accompanying graph
the accompanying map of the United States

Procedure

1. Carefully observe Figure 1, which shows a comparison of the difference in arrival time between P and S waves and distance to the epicenter of an earthquake. Note that the two quantities are directly related; that is, the greater the difference in arrival time, the greater the distance to the epicenter.

2. Before going further in this investigation, you will need to become familiar with the graph. Use the graph to answer questions 1 through 4 in Observations.

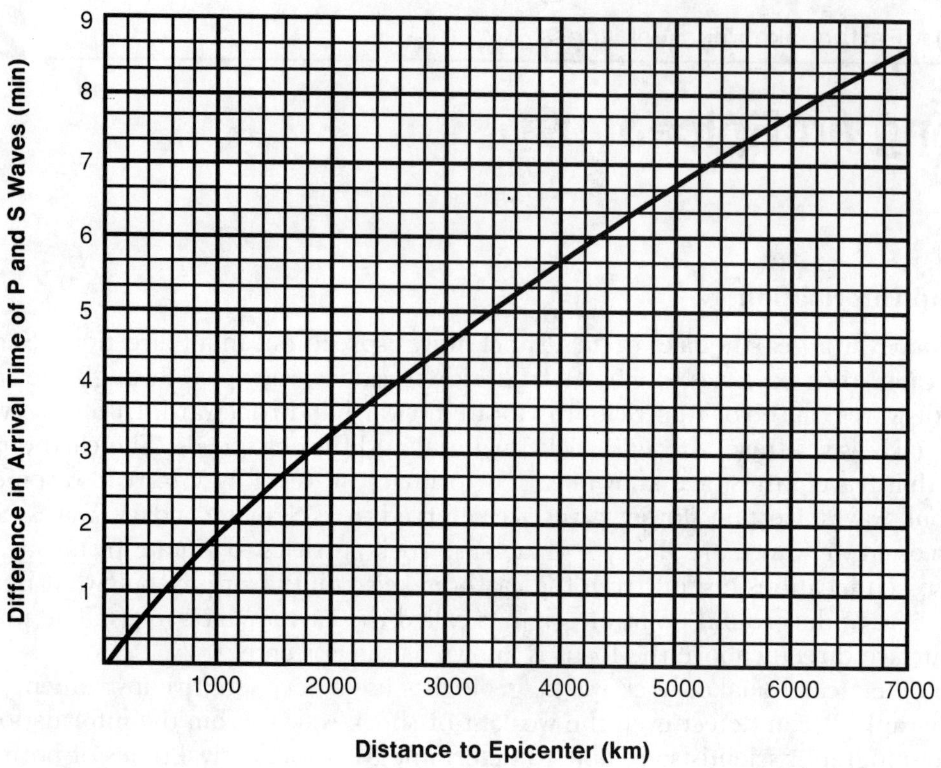

Figure 1

3. Now that you know how to read the graph, see if you can put it to use. Assume that an earthquake has occurred and that the times of arrival of the P and S waves from it have been detected and recorded by seismographs located at the three cities listed in the Data Table. Note that the difference in P and S wave arrival times has been included in the table.

4. Using Figure 1, determine each city's distance from the earthquake epicenter. Enter your figures in the Data Table.

5. Use the map scale to set your compass at a radius equal to the distance from Denver to the earthquake epicenter.

6. Draw a circle with the radius determined in step 5, using Denver as the center. Draw the circle on the map in Figure 2.

7. Repeat steps 5 and 6 for Houston and Miami.

8. If you have worked carefully, the three circles should intersect at one point. This point marks the epicenter of the earthquake.

Name ______________________ Class ____________ Date ________

Observations

DATA TABLE 1

City	Difference in P and S Wave Arrival Time	Distance (km)
Denver, Colorado	2 min 25 sec	
Houston, Texas	4 min 10 sec	
Miami, Florida	5 min 40 sec	

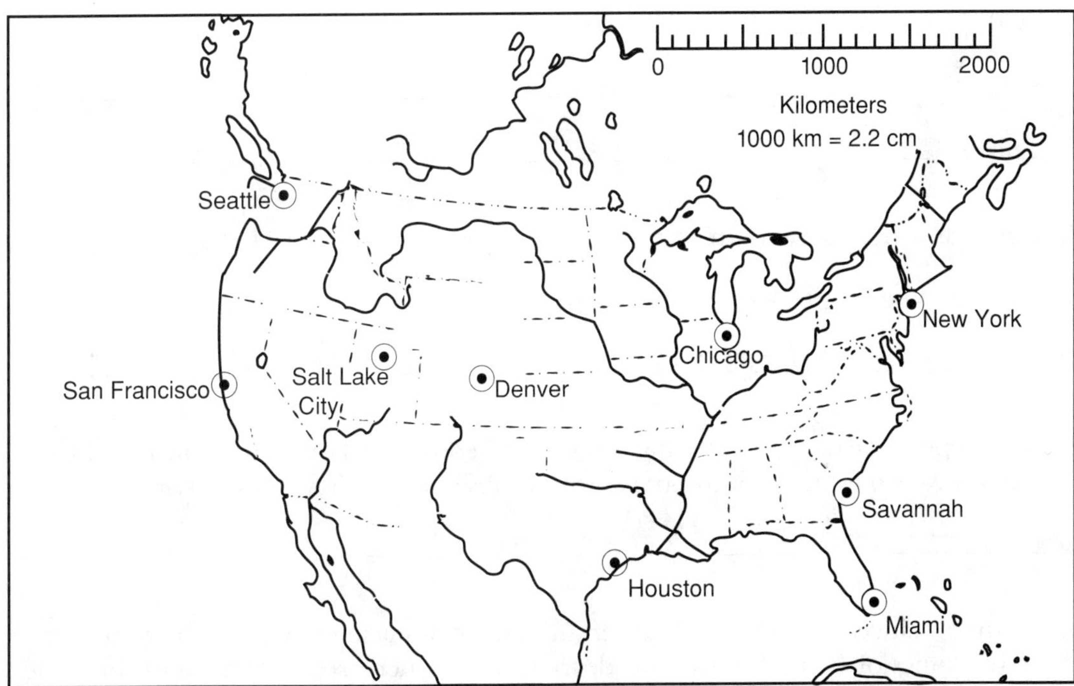

Figure 2

1. If the difference in arrival time for P and S waves at a certain location is 3 min, how far from that station is the epicenter? a. 430 km b. 1400 km c. 1800 km d. 2100 km
2. If a seismograph shows that a P wave arrives 7 min 20 sec before an S wave, how far is it to the earthquake's epicenter? ______________________

____

3. If a recording station is known to be 4600 km from an earthquake epicenter, what is the difference in arrival time between the P and S waves from that earthquake?

___

4. If a seismograph is located 2200 km from an earthquake epicenter, how great will be the difference in arrival time between the P and S waves at this station?

___

Analysis and Conclusions

1. a. Which city on the map is closest to the earthquake epicenter?

   ___

   b. How far, in km, is this city from the epicenter? ___

2. Which of the three cities listed in the Data Table would have become aware of the earthquake first? ___

   Second? ___

   Third? ___

3. Why was it necessary to know the distance from the epicenter for at least three recording stations to be able to locate the epicenter? ___

   ___

4. If the epicenter of this earthquake were located in San Francisco, how much earlier than the S wave would the P wave arrive for an observer in New York City?

   ___

5. As the distance between an observer and an earthquake decreases, the difference in arrival times of P and S waves a. decreases, b. increases, c. remains the same.

Critical Thinking and Application

1. What can happen to the Earth's surface when the vibrations from an earthquake travel through the crust? ___

   ___

   ___

   ___

2. What relationship do you think exists between the amount of energy an earthquake contains and the amount of damage it will do?

____

____

____

3. Is it possible for seismologists to know for sure that an earthquake or volcanic eruption will not occur in a particular area? Explain your answer.

____

____

____

Going Further

Find out about the construction of buildings in earthquake zones. Buildings in areas that have earthquakes are built with certain unique construction features. What do you think some of these features might be? You may want to write to the National Center for Earthquake Research, Geologic Survey Field Center, Menlo Park, CA 94025, and request some information about the construction of earthquake-proof buildings.

Name ________________ Class ________ Date ________

Laboratory Investigation

Chapter 11 Earthquakes and Volcanoes **25**

Investigating the Speed of Earthquake Waves

Background Information

When an earthquake occurs, waves are produced that travel outward away from the focus of the earthquake, in much the same way that ripples move across the surface of water when a pebble is thrown into a pond.

Primary waves and secondary waves are two different types of waves produced by an earthquake. They are usually referred to as P waves and S waves. The graphic relationship between how far P and S waves travel and the length of time that they have traveled is an important tool used by scientists who investigate earthquakes.

In this investigation you will construct a P and S wave travel-time graph. You will then use the graph to answer some questions about earthquakes.

Problem

What is an earthquake wave travel-time graph and how is it used?

Materials *(per group)*

pen or pencil

Procedure

1. An earthquake recently occurred producing P and S waves that were recorded by instruments located at the stations identified in the Data Table. The Data Table also indicates the distance traveled and the travel time for each wave. Using the information contained in the Data Table, construct a graph showing the relationship between the distance traveled by P and S waves and their travel time. There will be two slightly curved lines on your graph. Label the curves appropriately as either P wave or S wave.
2. Use the graph that you constructed to answer the questions in Analysis and Conclusions.

Observations

DATA TABLE

Wave Type	Distance Traveled from the epicenter (km)	Travel Time (min)	(sec)
P	1600	3	20
P	6500	9	50
P	5400	8	40
P	2000	4	00
P	9600	12	40
P	700	1	30
P	7000	10	20
P	3400	6	10
P	8800	12	00
P	4000	7	00
S	2200	8	00
S	4000	12	40
S	5200	15	20
S	1700	6	30
S	6000	17	00
S	1100	4	20
S	7400	19	40
S	8200	21	00
S	500	2	10
S	9000	22	10

Analysis and Conclusions

1. a. If an earthquake occurred near where you live, would P waves or S waves arrive at your location first? ______

b. Explain your answer. ______

2. a. How long would it take for a P wave to travel from an earthquake epicenter to a location 8000 km away? ______

b. How long would it take for an S wave to travel the same distance?

______

3. Approximately how far must an observer be from an earthquake epicenter if he or she received a P wave 8 minutes after it was produced by the earthquake?

______

4. Explain how you could tell which of two observers was farthest from an earthquake epicenter by comparing the arrival times of P and S waves for the two locations.

______

______

______

Name ________________ Class ________ Date ______

Earthquake S Wave and P Wave Travel-Time Graph

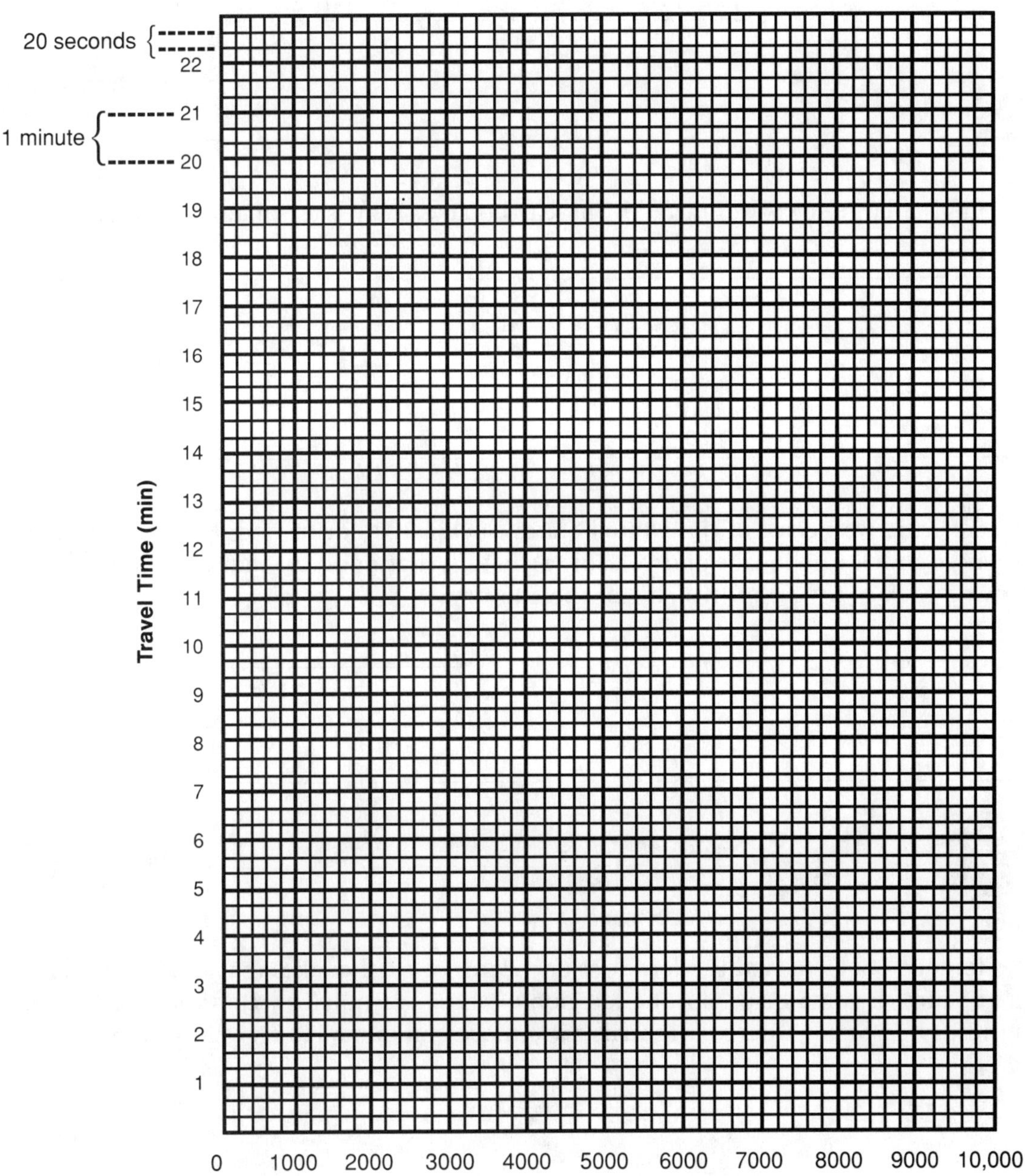

Critical Thinking and Application

1. How far from an earthquake epicenter would an observer be if he or she measured a difference of 8 minutes and 40 seconds in the arrival times of a P and S wave?

2. What kinds of landforms would you be most likely to find in an earthquake zone?

3. A tsunami is a large sea wave started by an earthquake. Why is a tsunami so dangerous?

4. States along the west coast of the United States, such as California and Washington, have experienced much earthquake and volcanic activity. What does this indicate about the underlying rock structure of this part of the country?

Going Further

Use reference books to find the locations and dates of earthquakes that have occurred in the United States. Using a map, plot the location of these earthquakes. Do there seem to be areas in the United States where earthquakes are more common? How would you explain this?

Name ______________________ Class ____________ Date ________

Laboratory Investigation

Chapter 12 Plate Tectonics **26**

Observing Convection Currents

Background Information

Many scientists think that there are convection currents of hot rock within the mantle of the Earth. They think that the hot rock rises and flows out along the ridges. As this process goes on along the ridges, new ocean floor is created that pushes older ocean floor toward the continents. These scientists think that the continents are gradually moving because of these convection currents.

In this investigation you will construct a working model of a convection current and study its action.

Problem

How can a model of a convection current be prepared and used to illustrate ocean-floor spreading?

Materials *(per group)*

400-mL beaker
Bunsen burner or candle
ring stand
food coloring
sawdust
beaker clamp

Procedure

1. Fill the beaker about three-fourths full with water.
2. Place the beaker into the beaker clamp and attach the clamp to the ring stand. See Figure 1.

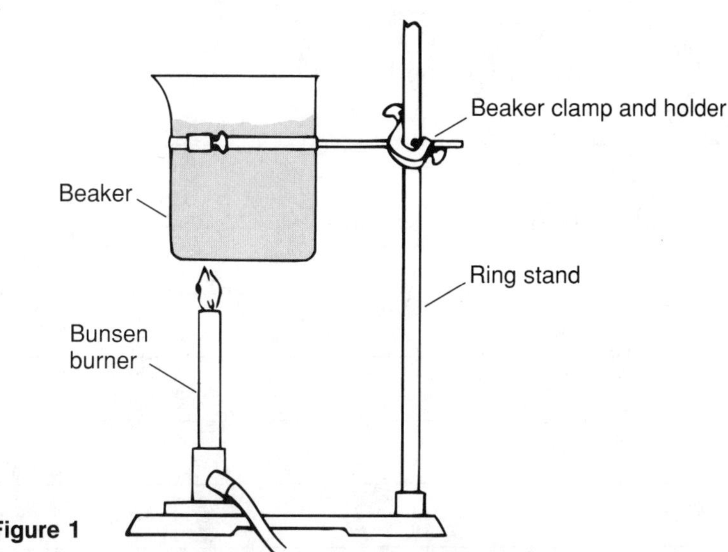

Figure 1

3. Light and adjust the flame on the burner you are using.

4. Adjust the beaker on the ring stand so that the flame of the burner is directly heating only one side of the beaker.

5. When the water just begins to boil, add a few drops of food coloring. Draw arrows in Figure 2 to show the path of the food coloring.

6. Turn off the burner and allow the water in the beaker to cool a little. Carefully sprinkle a fine layer of sawdust over the surface of the water.

7. Relight your burner and adjust the flame. Heat one side of the beaker as you did in step 4.

8. Observe what happens to the sawdust as you look from above.

9. Turn off your burner. Allow your apparatus to cool completely before dismantling it.

Observations

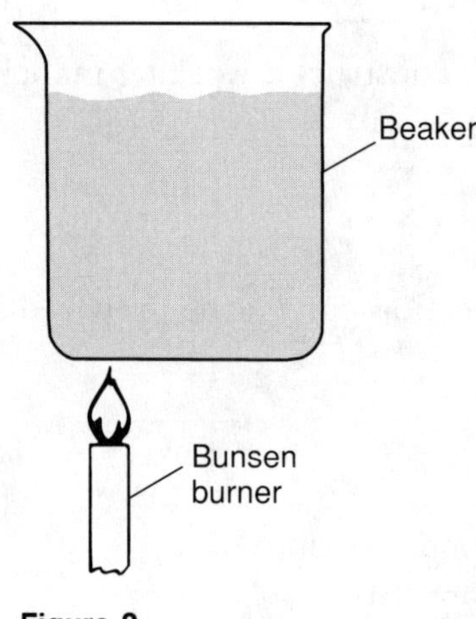

Figure 2

Analysis and Conclusions

1. Explain the pattern formed by the food coloring.

____

____

2. Where was "new" water constantly being brought to the surface?

____

3. Describe and explain the motion of the sawdust.

____

____

____

____

____

Name ______________________ Class ____________ Date ________

Critical Thinking and Application

1. How does the model you prepared compare to convection currents in the Earth's interior?

____

____

____

____

2. If two moving continents collided as a result of the convection currents that occurred beneath them, what changes might occur on the surface of the continents?

____

____

____

3. Why is it important for scientists to know where plate boundaries are located?

____

____

____

Going Further

Make a large diagram of how a convection current might work deep under the ocean floor. Use posterboard, crayons, colored pencils, and paint.

Name ______ Class ______ Date ______

Laboratory Investigation

Identifying Common Minerals

Background Information

Scientists have identified more than 2000 different kinds of minerals. However, most minerals are very rare. Over 95 percent of the Earth's crust is made of rocks that are composed of about a dozen minerals. These common minerals are called rock-forming minerals. While minerals can vary a great deal in their chemical makeup and the forms in which they are found, most common minerals can be identified by observing a few of their basic properties.

In this investigation you will observe the physical properties of some common rock-forming minerals and use these properties to identify the minerals. To do so, you will have to test for the physical properties described below.

SOME PHYSICAL PROPERTIES OF MINERALS

Hardness is the resistance of a mineral to scratching. A mineral will scratch any other substance less hard than itself.

Table of Hardness of Common Items

Item	Approximate Hardness
Fingernail	2.5
Copper penny	3.0
Steel nail	5.5
Glass	6.0

Streak is the color of a fine powder of a mineral. Rubbing a mineral against a piece of dull tile, or streak plate, will powder enough of the mineral to enable you to determine its streak.

Cleavage is the quality of a mineral that causes it to split, leaving smooth, flat surfaces. When a mineral does not split to leave smooth, flat surfaces, the break is called a fracture. You can easily observe whether a mineral shows cleavage or fracture.

Minerals have a characteristic *crystal shape*. A crystal is a solid that has flat surfaces, or faces, arranged in a definite shape. There are six crystal systems, or categories of crystal shapes: cubic, hexagonal, orthorhombic, monoclinic, tetragonal, and triclinic. Most minerals belong to only one crystal system. A few, however, belong to more than one system. Serpentine crystals, for example, may be monoclinic, orthorhombic, or hexagonal. Although the crystals in each system share certain basic mathematical characteristics, they may appear quite different from one another. Consider three minerals whose crystals belong to the cubic system: halite, diamond, and garnet. Halite crystals, which are shaped like tiny cubes, have six square faces. Diamond crystals have eight triangular faces. And garnet crystals have twelve faces, each of which has five sides.

Luster is the way a mineral reflects light. Minerals may be described as having metallic or nonmetallic luster. Metallic luster is the shine associated with a freshly polished metal surface. Nonmetallic luster may be described by terms such as glassy, brilliant, or greasy.

Density is the mass, per unit volume of a substance. Density can be estimated by determining a sample's heft, or how heavy it seems for its size. Samples that seem heavy for their size are described as dense, while samples that seem light for their size are described as not very dense.

Some minerals have *special properties* that can be used to identify them. For example, a few minerals are magnetic and will be attracted to a magnet.

Problem

How can the physical properties of minerals be used to identify them?

Materials *(per group)*

set of common mineral samples
magnet
piece of dull tile (streak plate)
hardness kit containing a
copper penny, a steel nail, and
a piece of glass (scratch plate)

Procedure

Carefully test and observe each mineral sample to determine its physical characteristics. Use the summary of mineral physical properties in the Mineral Identification Key on the next page. Enter your observations in the appropriate space in the Data Table.

Name ____________________ Class __________ Date __________

Mineral Identification Key

Directions: Determine the identity of your samples by comparing their properties with the descriptions listed in the key. Start at the left and work to the right while progressively narrowing the possibilities.

Luster / Color	Streak / Hardness	Cleavage	Description	Mineral
Metallic luster	Black, green-black or dark green streak		Black; strongly magnetic; hardness, 6	Magnetite
			Lead-pencil black; smudges fingers; hardness, 1 to 2	Graphite
			Brass yellow; cubic crystals; hardness, 6 to 6.5	Pyrite
			Brass yellow, may be tarnished purple; hardness, 3.5 to 4	Chalcopyrite
			Shiny gray; very heavy; cubic cleavage; hardness, 2.5	Galena
	Brown or white streak		Yellow-brown to dark brown, may be almost black; hardness, 5 to 5.5	Limonite
			Yellow-brown; streak white to pale yellow; resinous luster; hardness, 3.5 to 4	Sphalerite
			Red to brown streak; hardness 5.5 to 6.5	Hematite
Nonmetallic, light-colored	Scratches glass	Cleavage	Pink to bluish gray to green; 2 cleavage planes at right angles; hardness, 6	Orthoclase
		No cleavage	Glassy luster; crystals are 6-sided when present; hardness, 7; shell-like fracture	Quartz
			Glassy luster; shades of green and yellow; hardness, 6.5 to 7	Olivine
	Does not scratch glass	Cleavage	Colorless to white; salty taste; cubic cleavage; hardness, 2.5	Halite
			White or yellow to colorless; hardness, 3; double image seen when crystal is placed on printed page	Calcite
			White to transparent; hardness, 2	Gypsum
			Green to white; feels soapy; hardness, 1	Talc
			Colorless to light yellow; hardness, 2 to 2.5; cleavage in flat sheets	Muscovite
			White, yellow, purple, or green; 8-sided cleavage; hardness, 4	Fluorite
Nonmetallic, dark-colored	Scratches glass	Cleavage	Black; cleavage with 2 planes at 90° angles; hardness, 5 to 6	Augite
			Black; cleavage with 2 planes at 60° angles; hardness, 5 to 6	Hornblende
		No cleavage	Gray, brown, blue-gray, pink, white, red; 6-sided crystals; hardness, 9	Corundum
			Reddish brown; fracture resembles poor cleavage; brittle; hardness 6.5 to 7.5	Garnet
	Does not scratch glass	Cleavage	Brown to black; hardness 2.5 to 3	Biotite
			Shades of green; hardness, 2 to 2.5	Chlorite
		No cleavage	Green, brown, blue, or purple; shell-like fracture; hardness, 5	Apatite

Observations

DATA TABLE

Mineral Number	Color	Streak Color	Luster (Check One)		The Mineral Shows: (Check One)		Hardness (Check One)			Other Observed Properties	Mineral Name
			Metallic	Nonmetallic	Cleavage	Fracture	Less Than 2.5	2.5–6.0	More Than 6.0		

Name ______________________ Class ____________ Date ________

Analysis and Conclusions

Using the Mineral Identification Key and your observations in the Data Table, identify each mineral and enter its name in the Data Table.

Critical Thinking and Application

1. According to the Mineral Identification Key, what is the only physical property that can be used to distinguish between pyrite and chalcopyrite, assuming that both minerals are the same color?

   ____

2. What are the two softest minerals listed in the Mineral Identification Key?

   ____

3. What is the hardest mineral listed in the Mineral Identification Key? What must then be true about this mineral? ______________________________

   ____

4. Which physical property is the least helpful in identifying minerals? The most helpful?

   ____

   ____

5. Explain the following statement: You can determine the identity of a mineral by showing what it *cannot* be. ______________________________

   ____

   ____

   ____

Going Further

Collect mineral samples from around your school or home. Perform the mineral characteristics tests on your samples. Then see if you can identify each sample.

Name ______________________ Class ____________ Date ________

Laboratory Investigation

Chapter 13 Rocks and Minerals **28**

Calculating the Specific Gravity of Minerals

Background Information

One of the most important properties of a mineral is specific gravity. Specific gravity is the ratio of the mass of a substance to the mass of an equal volume of water. Specific gravity is an important property of a substance because it is always the same regardless of the size of the sample tested. Therefore, specific gravity can be very useful when trying to identify minerals.

Archimedes, a Greek scientist, discovered that when an object is submerged in water, the mass of the water displaced by the object is equal to the apparent loss of mass of the object in the water. This principle can be used to determine specific gravity.

In this investigation you will learn a way to determine specific gravity and you will use it to determine the specific gravity of three minerals. Then you will use your data to identify an unknown mineral.

Problem

How can you determine specific gravity? How can you use specific gravity to identify minerals?

Materials *(per group)*

thread
spring scale (grams)
ring stand
burette clamp
250-mL beaker
pyrite, quartz, and galena samples
unknown sample

Procedure

1. Tie a length of thread firmly to the sample of pyrite. Attach the other end of the thread to the spring scale. Suspend the spring scale from the burette clamp so that the pyrite is about 5 cm from the table. See Figure 1. Record the mass of the sample in the Data Table.

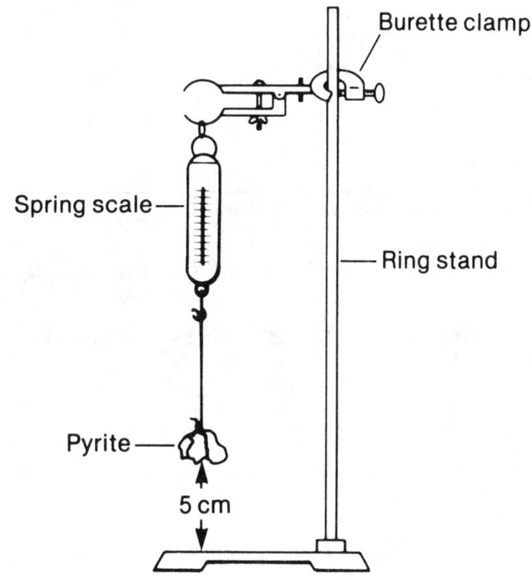

Figure 1

2. Fill the beaker three-quarters full with water. Place the beaker of water under the spring scale so that the pyrite is completely covered by the water but not touching the sides or the bottom of the beaker. Record the apparent mass in water in the Data Table.

3. Calculate the apparent loss of mass by subtracting the apparent mass in water from the mass in air. Record your answer in the Data Table.

4. The apparent loss of mass of pyrite you just calculated is equal to the mass of water displaced. Record this in the Data Table.

5. Calculate the specific gravity of pyrite. Record your answer in the Data Table.

$$\text{Specific gravity} = \frac{\text{mass of the mineral in air}}{\text{mass of water displaced by the mineral}}$$

6. Repeat steps 1 through 5 for quartz and galena. Record your answers in the Data Table.

7. Obtain an unknown mineral sample from your teacher. It has been covered with paint to disguise the color. Find the specific gravity and record it in the Data Table.

Observations

DATA TABLE	Pyrite	Quartz	Galena	Unknown Sample
Mass in air				
Apparent mass in water				
Apparent loss of mass in water				
Mass of water displaced				
Specific gravity				

Analysis and Conclusions

1. Which mineral has the highest specific gravity? The lowest?

____

2. How many times larger than a piece of galena would a piece of quartz have to be in order to have the same mass? Explain. _______________

____

____

3. What is the identity of the unknown sample? How can you tell?

____

____

____

Name ______________________ Class ____________ Date ________

Critical Thinking and Application

1. Why would you not use specific gravity alone to identify minerals?

____

____

____

2. Pyrite is sometimes called "fool's gold" because its color and appearance are similar to real gold. How could a scientist determine if a sample was real gold?

____

____

3. How could a jeweler determine if a sample was pure gold mixed with some other metal?

____

____

4. Explain how specific gravity and density are related.

____

____

____

____

____

5. Based on your answer to question 4, explain why specific gravity is a number with no units. ____

____

____

____

____

Going Further

Try to determine the specific gravity of a substance that floats and a substance that dissolves in water. Devise a way to determine the specific gravity of a piece of ice or a cork. Devise a way to determine the specific gravity of rock candy or halite.

Name ______________________ Class ____________ Date ____________

Laboratory Investigation

Chapter 13 Rocks and Minerals **29**

Classifying Rocks

Background Information

The Earth's crust is made of rocks. Scientists place all rocks in categories called classes according to the way the rocks were formed. The three major classes of rocks are sedimentary rocks, igneous rocks, and metamorphic rocks. Rocks from each class tend to show characteristics that are the result of the conditions that existed at the time they were formed. Using these characteristics, almost any rock sample can be identified as belonging to one of the three classes.

In this investigation you will examine several rock samples. Then, given a list of some of the major characteristics of the three classes, you will place each rock sample in the proper class. Below you will find lists of some of the more common characteristics of each class of rock.

Characteristics of Sedimentary Rocks

1. Most sedimentary rocks are composed of fragments of other rocks that look very much like sediment. Some sedimentary rocks have a range of particle sizes, while other sedimentary rocks consist mainly of one sediment size. See Figure 1.

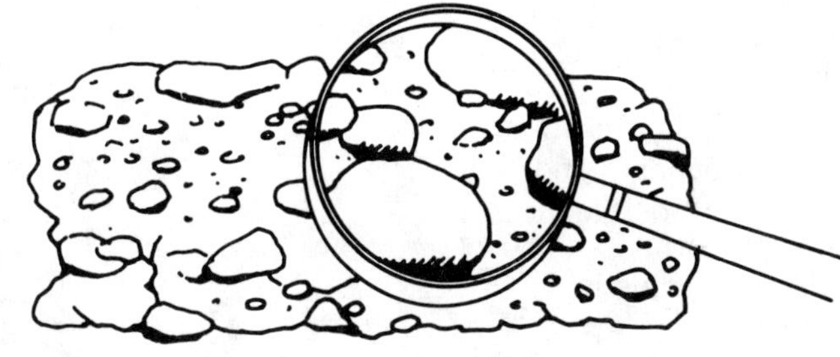

Figure 1

2. Some sedimentary rocks are of organic origin; that is, they are composed of plant and animal products or remains. Such rocks often contain fossils. See Figure 2.

Figure 2

3. Sedimentary rocks often have distinct parallel layers. See Figure 3.

4. Sedimentary rocks often appear dull or earthy.

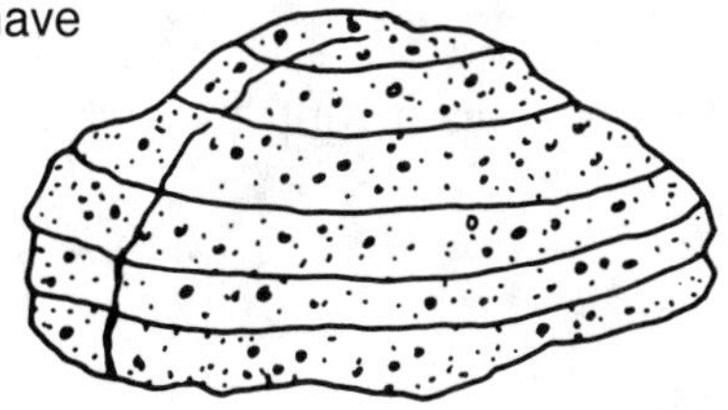

Figure 3

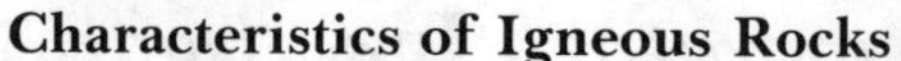

Characteristics of Igneous Rocks

1. Igneous rocks may contain crystals, which frequently can be seen by the unaided eye. See Figure 4.
2. Some igneous rocks (those that cooled rapidly) contain no crystals and therefore appear glassy. See Figure 5.
3. Igneous rocks may be found in many colors and often show different-colored crystals that are not in bands.

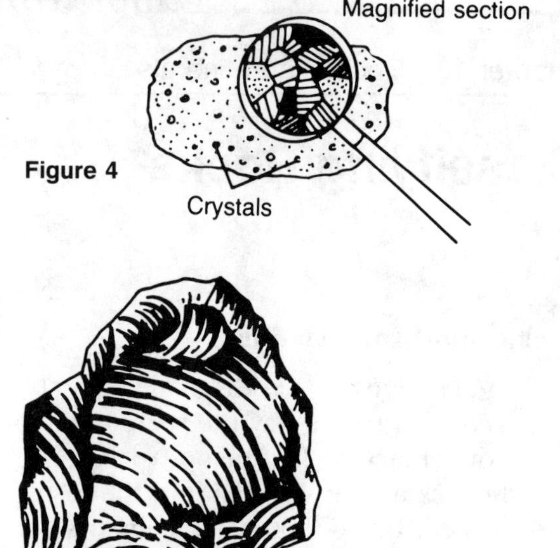

Figure 4

Figure 5

Characteristics of Metamorphic Rocks

1. Metamorphic rocks often may look like igneous rocks except that they do show bands of color. See Figure 6.
2. Metamorphic rocks may show signs of bending and distortion. See Figure 7.
3. Mineral crystals in metamorphic rocks will generally be flattened.

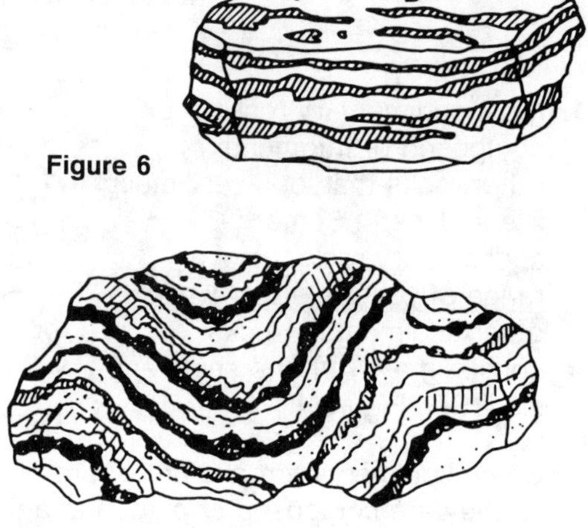

Figure 6

Figure 7

Problem

How can rock samples be identified according to rock class?

Materials *(per group)*

set of natural rock samples
magnifying glass

Procedure

1. Select one of the numbered rock samples provided by your teacher and examine it carefully.

2. After you have determined the sample's most obvious physical properties, compare them to the lists of major characteristics for each of the three classes of rock.

3. Select the rock class that contains descriptions of rocks having properties that best fit the characteristics of the sample you have just observed.

4. Place a check in the box in the Data Table that properly identifies the class your rock sample seems to fit. In the space provided, list the characteristics possessed by your sample that guided you toward your decision. Notice that information describing rock sample A has been completed for you. This will serve as a model or aid toward proper completion of this investigation.

5. Repeat the above procedure for each of the samples provided.

Observations

Complete the Data Table on page 140.

Analysis and Conclusions

1. List three physical properties that help to identify a given rock sample as a sedimentary rock. ________________

____

____

2. List three physical properties that help to identify a given rock sample as an igneous rock.

____

____

____

3. List three physical properties that help to identify a given rock sample as a metamorphic rock. ________________

____

____

DATA TABLE

	Rock Class			Description
Sample A	Sed.	Ig.	Meta.	This rock has lots of little sparkling particles that look like crystals. There are four different colors of crystals and they are not bands of color.
		√		
Sample 1	Sed.	Ig.	Meta.	
Sample 2	Sed.	Ig.	Meta.	
Sample 3	Sed.	Ig.	Meta.	
Sample 4	Sed.	Ig.	Meta.	
Sample 5	Sed.	Ig.	Meta.	
Sample 6	Sed.	Ig.	Meta.	
Sample 7	Sed.	Ig.	Meta.	
Sample 8	Sed.	Ig.	Meta.	
Sample 9	Sed.	Ig.	Meta.	
Sample 10	Sed.	Ig.	Meta.	
Sample 11	Sed.	Ig.	Meta.	
Sample 12	Sed.	Ig.	Meta.	

Name ______ Class ______ Date ______

Critical Thinking and Application

1. A fossil is the preserved remains or evidence of an ancient living thing. Explain why fossils are rarely found in igneous or metamorphic rocks.

2. Why might metamorphic rocks show signs of bending and distortion?

3. Why might metamorphic rocks be more likely to show bands of color than igneous rocks?

Going Further

Collect various kinds of rocks from your neighborhood. Use the descriptions given in this investigation to classify as many different samples as you can.

Relating Cooling Rate and Crystal Size

Background Information

All rocks are made up of one or more minerals. Some rocks are formed from molten rock. When molten rock cools and hardens, it forms igneous rocks. Igneous rocks may contain crystals. The size of the crystals depends upon how quickly the molten rock that forms the igneous rocks cools. Some igneous rocks do not have crystals, while others may have small or large crystals.

In this investigation you will form crystals from melted material. You will observe how the cooling rate affects the size of the crystals that are formed.

Problem

How does cooling rate affect the size of crystals?

Materials *(per group)*

3 glass caster cups
3 small test tubes
test-tube holder
paradichlorobenzene (PDB) flakes
hot plate
magnifying glass
glass-marking pencil
crushed ice
500-mL beaker
400-mL beaker
150-mL beaker
tongs
paper towels
rock samples of rhyolite, granite, and obsidian

Procedure

1. Fill the 400-mL beaker three-quarters full with water. Place a caster cup in the beaker. Boil the water on the hot plate. **CAUTION:** *Observe safety procedures when using a hot plate.*
2. Fill the 500-mL beaker with crushed ice. Place the second caster cup in the beaker. Leave the third caster cup at room temperature.
3. Fill each of the three small test tubes with paradichlorobenzene (PDB) flakes.

4. Half fill the 150-mL beaker with water. Place the three test tubes in the beaker. Place the beaker with the test tubes on the hot plate. **CAUTION:** *Work in a well-ventilated room.* Heat the beaker gently until the paradichlorobenzene melts.
5. Using the tongs, carefully remove the caster cup from the boiling water. Have your partner quickly dry the cup. Using the test-tube holder, remove one test tube from the beaker. Pour the PDB in this test tube into the caster cup. Time how long it takes for the PDB to completely become a solid. Label the caster cup A and record the time in the Data Table.
6. Remove the second caster cup from the beaker with ice and dry it quickly and completely. Using the test-tube holder, pour the second test tube of PDB into this cup. Time how long it takes for the PDB to completely turn solid. Label this cup B and record the time in the Data Table.
7. Using the test-tube holder, pour the third test tube of PDB into the caster cup at room temperature. Again, time how long it takes for this PDB to completely turn solid. Label this caster cup C and record the time in the Data Table.
8. Look at the contents of each caster cup with the magnifying glass. Draw the contents of each caster cup in the spaces provided in Observations.
9. Look at the crystals in the samples of rhyolite, granite, and obsidian with a magnifying glass. Draw the crystals in each sample in the spaces provided in Observations.

Observations

DATA TABLE

Caster Cup	Time
A	
B	
C	

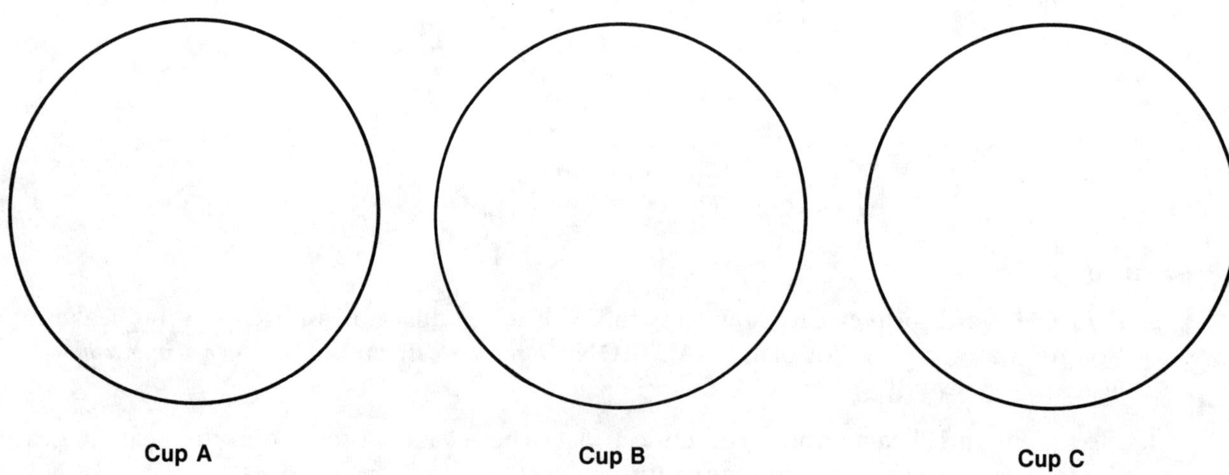

Cup A Cup B Cup C

Name ______________________ Class ____________ Date ________

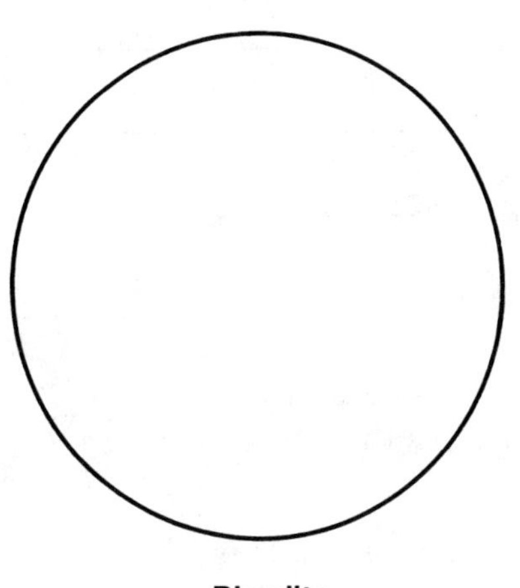

Rhyolite

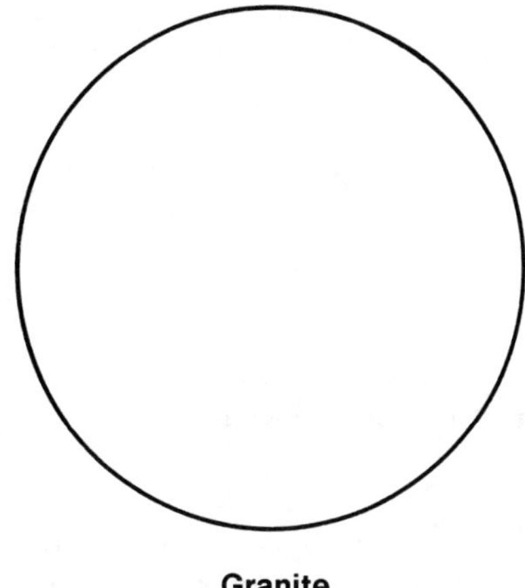

Granite

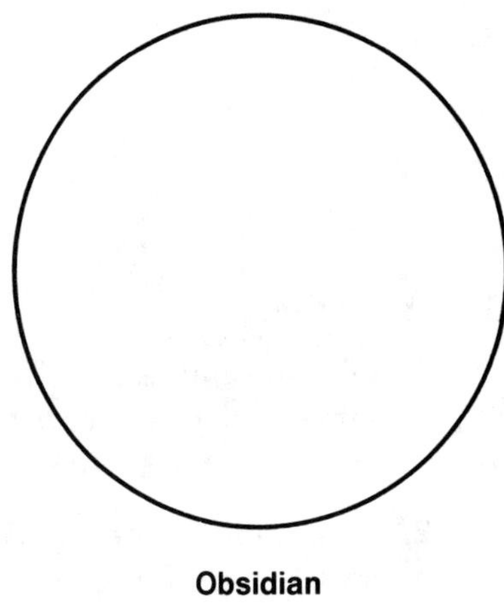

Obsidian

Analysis and Conclusions

1. Compare the crystals in the caster cups to the samples of granite, rhyolite, and obsidian. Which PDB crystals are most similar to the crystals in the rock samples?

____

____

2. How does the rate of cooling affect the size of crystals?

____

____

3. Granite, rhyolite, and obsidian are essentially made of the same materials. Explain why they look different.

____

____

Critical Thinking and Application

1. Where would igneous rocks have a chance to cool slowly?

____

____

2. Where would igneous rocks cool rapidly?

____

____

3. In general, if you saw a rock that contained large, interlocking crystals, what would you conclude about the way it formed?

____

____

____

Going Further

1. Obtain samples of obsidian, granite, and pumice. These three rocks are made of the same minerals. Describe their appearances. What are some reasons that these rocks appear so different?
2. Pour some melted PDB flakes directly into ice water. Examine the results. Does this mostly resemble pumice, obsidian, or granite in the way it was formed? Explain your answer.

Name ________________ Class ________ Date ________

Laboratory Investigation

Chapter 14 Weathering and Soil Formation **31**

Investigating Rock Abrasion

Background Information

Substances on the Earth are constantly undergoing change. One type of change occurs when rocks are broken into smaller pieces and then rounded as they are moved about in rivers and streams. This kind of change is known as a physical change. The process of rubbing and bumping together that causes this kind of physical change is called abrasion.

In this investigation you will observe the physical changes that rocks undergo through the process of abrasion in a model situation.

Problem

What effect does length of time of abrasion have on the way rock particles weather?

Materials *(per group)*

bottle, jar, or can with lid
presoaked rock chips
triple-beam balance
screen
clock or timer

Procedure

1. Obtain a sample of presoaked rock chips and drain them to remove excess water. **Note:** *Place the rocks on the screen so that they do not get lost.*
2. Use the balance to measure out 100 g of rock from your sample. Return the extra pieces to the supply container.
3. Place the 100 g of chips in the container provided.
4. Add water to the container until it is about half full. Close the lid tightly over the container. Shake the container at a constant rate for 3 minutes.
5. Carefully pour the water from the container into a sink. Use the screen to make sure not even the smallest rock piece is lost.
6. Measure the mass of the chips again and record your result in the Data Table.
7. Return the rock chips to the container, close the container, and repeat steps 4 through 6 four more times. Record the results after each 3 minutes of shaking, for a total of 15 minutes.
8. Graph the results, comparing mass remaining with time of shaking.

Observations

DATA TABLE

Weathering Time (min)	Mass of Rock Remaining (g)
0	100
3	
6	
9	
12	
15	

GRAPH

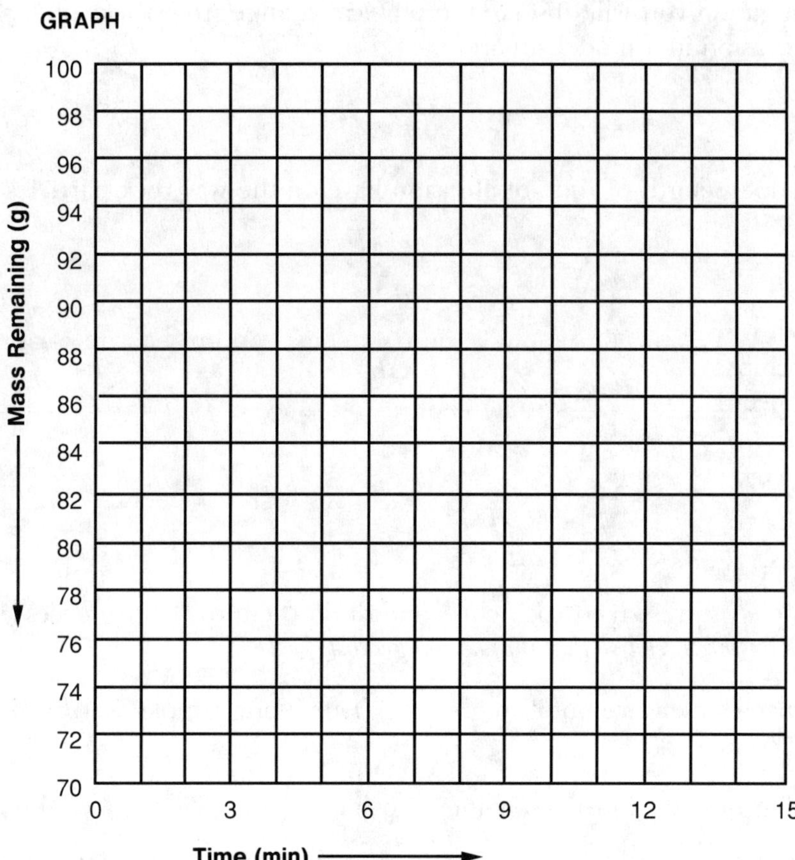

Analysis and Conclusions

1. Why were the rock chips presoaked before you used them? ______________________

____

2. As you examined the rock pieces after each shaking period, how did the amount of rounding change as the abrasion time increased? ______________________

____

3. From your data in the Data Table, describe how the mass remaining changed through time. ______________________

4. Did the difference in mass remaining at the end of each shaking period change in a regular manner? ______________________

Explain why you think the mass remaining changed in the way that it did.

____

____

____

5. What do you think might happen to the rate (speed) at which the rock chips were being worn away if you continued to shake them for an hour?

____

____

6. What effect do you think the shape of the rock chips had on the rate of abrasion?

____

____

Critical Thinking and Application

1. How do you think the hardness of a rock would affect the rate at which it would weather? ______________________

____

____

2. Do you think the rate at which water moves over a rock affects how rapidly the rock weathers? Explain your answer. ______________________

____

____

____

3. The pyramids that were built thousands of years ago in the deserts of Egypt have experienced some weathering due to abrasion. What do you think is responsible for this abrasion? ______________________________

____

____

____

Going Further

Repeat the procedure with rock salt (halite) chips of the same size. Describe any differences in the rate of abrasion that you observed between the halite and the rock chips that you used the first time. Explain why you think the rock salt weathered in the way that it did.

Name ______________________ Class ____________ Date ________

Laboratory Investigation

Chapter 14 Weathering and Soil Formation **32**

Observing the Effects of Chemical Weathering on Chalk

Background Information

Rocks are gradually broken apart into smaller and smaller pieces by weathering. Weathering is caused by wind, water, or other natural forces. Sometimes weathering is caused by chemical reactions. One important factor that affects the rate of chemical weathering is the size of the particles.

In this investigation you will observe the relationship between particle size and reaction rate. This investigation will also help you understand how a form of chemical weathering works in nature.

Problem

How does the size of particles affect the rate of chemical weathering?

Materials *(per group)*

2 250-mL beakers
100 mL of dilute hydrochloric acid
2 pieces of classroom chalk
triple-beam balance
2 fine food strainers
paper towels

Procedure

1. Carefully pour 100 mL of dilute hydrochloric acid into each beaker. **CAUTION:** *Be careful not to spill acid on your clothing or skin. If you accidentally spill any acid on your clothing or skin, wash immediately with water.*
2. Using the triple-beam balance, find the mass of each piece of chalk. Record the masses in the Data Table. They should be about the same.
3. Break one piece of chalk into several small pieces.
4. Simultaneously place the broken chalk and the unbroken chalk into the two beakers of acid. Observe what happens.
5. Wait a few minutes. Pour the contents of one beaker through one strainer. Pour the contents of the other beaker through the second strainer. Allow the acid to go into the sink. Gently run the water for a minute or two.

6. Gently dry both samples of chalk with paper towels.
7. Find the mass of each sample of chalk. Record the masses in the Data Table. Calculate the amount of chalk that reacted in each beaker and complete the Data Table.

Observations

DATA TABLE

Setup	Masses	
	Whole Piece of Chalk	Broken Pieces
Mass before being placed in acid		
Mass after being placed in acid		
Amount of chalk that reacted with the acid		

Analysis and Conclusions

1. In which beaker did the reaction proceed more rapidly?

____

____

2. Besides the difference in mass, how else could you tell that one reaction was faster than the other? ____

____

____

3. In which beaker was more surface area of chalk exposed to the acid?

____

____

4. In nature, which would weather more rapidly—a 10-kg piece of limestone or 10 1-kg pieces? Why? ____

____

____

Name ______________________ Class __________ Date ________

Critical Thinking and Application

1. In order to burn fuel oil more efficiently, some companies are selling a device that sprays the oil into the burner in a fine mist. Do you think this is a good idea? Explain your answer. ______________________

2. If flour is in a bag, it is very hard to ignite. However, bakeries will not permit flames in rooms where flour dust may be in the air. They fear an explosion. Why should they be so careful? ______________________

3. How might a layer of topsoil protect a rock layer from chemical weathering?

4. Why might chemical weathering occur more rapidly in a highly populated city?

Going Further

Test some other substances to see how surface area affects their rate of chemical weathering. Obtain an iron nail and an equal mass of steel wool. Place each in an equal amount of water. Carefully observe the amount of rusting that takes place over several days.

Investigating the Composition of Soil

Background Information

All of the soil on the Earth was formed by the weathering of parent rock material. Organic matter in the form of humus that was added to the uppermost portion of the soil produced a rich, dark-colored topsoil. Centuries of rainfall carried materials downward from the topsoil, where they were trapped in the lower regions of the soil and produced subsoil.

In this investigation you will observe samples taken from the topsoil, subsoil, and parent material near where you live. You will study the characteristics of these samples to learn more about the processes that produced the soils in your area.

Problem

Of what is soil made?

Materials *(per group)*

samples of topsoil, subsoil, and parent material
magnifying glass
teasing needle
small test tube with stopper
sheet of white, unlined paper
metric ruler

Procedure

1. Using your ruler, draw two square shapes side by side on the sheet of unlined paper. Make each square approximately 5 cm on a side. Label one square "Topsoil" and the other square "Subsoil."

2. Place a small quantity of topsoil and subsoil on the sheet in the appropriate square.

3. Carefully observe the soil particles through the magnifying glass. Use the teasing needle to separate the particles. In the Data Table, list all characteristics of the topsoil and subsoil you can observe. Include such properties as color, particle size, and presence or absence of humus.

4. Carefully observe the sample of parent material, both with and without the magnifying glass.

5. You have learned that rainwater carries tiny soil particles downward from the topsoil into the subsoil. Many of the particles are too small to be seen with the unaided eye. These particles are called colloids. There is a simple test to detect colloids in soil. Place a small sample of soil, approximately a teaspoonful, in a test tube. Add water until the tube is about half-full. Place the stopper securely in the opening and shake the contents vigorously. Stop shaking the tube and allow the contents to settle for 2 or 3 minutes. If colloids are present, they will be so small that they will not settle quickly. They will give the water a cloudy look. Test the subsoil and topsoil for the presence of colloids.

6. Carefully replace the unused portions of your samples and clean up your work area.

Observations

DATA TABLE

Characteristics of Topsoil	Characteristics of Subsoil

1. How did the color of the topsoil and subsoil compare? ______________________

____

____

____

____

____

____

____

2. a. Did you find pieces of organic material in any of the three samples?

____

b. Which sample contained the most organic material? ______________________

3. a. Were there any pieces of minerals present in either of the two soil samples?

(Mineral particles will appear as small shiny pieces of various colors.) __________

b. Did you find any of the same minerals in the sample of parent material? __________

____

4. When you placed the soil samples in water and shook them, the particles should have settled in a particular order.

a. Which particles settled first? __________

b. Which particles settled last? __________

c. Which particles did not settle? __________

Analysis and Conclusions

1. In what ways is the parent material similar to the soil?

____

____

2. In what ways is the parent material different from the soil?

____

____

3. Did you find indications that there were colloids present in your samples of topsoil and subsoil? Explain your answer. __________

____

____

____

4. In some locations, soils were not formed from the parent material below them. Instead, they were formed somewhere else and were carried to their present location by winds, running water, or glaciers. If your soils were formed somewhere else and transported to your area, they will probably not resemble the parent rock material from your location. Based on your observations, do you think your soil formed from local parent material, or was it formed somewhere else and transported to your area? On what evidence do you base your answer? __________

____

____

Critical Thinking and Application

1. How does soil texture relate to weathering? ______

2. What do you think is responsible for the differences in color found in topsoil samples collected from various parts of the United States? ______

3. Is it possible to artificially increase the fertility of topsoil in a certain area? Explain your answer. ______

4. In which of the four climatic regions—arid, semiarid, subhumid, humid—would you expect to find the richest topsoil? Explain your answer. ______

Going Further

Test several different types of soil in your neighborhood or around the school. For example, collect soils from places that are particularly sandy or rocky. Repeat the above investigations using the soils that you collect.

Laboratory Investigation

Chapter 14 Weathering and Soil Formation **34**

A Closer Look at Soil

Background Information

Billions of kilograms of topsoil wash toward the ocean every year. Much of the erosion results from human actions, such as cutting down forests, allowing animals to graze too much, and growing one crop over and over in the same field.

When topsoil is lost, agriculture suffers. But the loss of topsoil has another important effect. It upsets the delicate balance between living things and natural resources. Many species of living things make the soil their home. Without soil, these organisms and their contributions to other living things disappear from a region.

In this investigation you will discover what organisms are present in soil.

Problem

What kind of plant and animal life can be found in a sample of topsoil and subsoil taken from ground near your school?

Materials *(per group)*

small hand shovel or digging tool
6 plastic bags, with elastic or wires for closing
3 paper cups
3 paper plates
white tray or large sheet of white paper
small sieve
microscope
medicine dropper
microscope slides and coverslips
magnifying glass
forceps
12 to 16 small glass jars with lids
clean sand
30 radish seeds or other fast-germinating seeds (soaked overnight in water)
metric ruler

Procedure

1. Decide as a class where to look outdoors for soil samples.
2. Your group should collect a sample of soil about 30 × 30 × 30 cm. Use a metric ruler to measure the plot. Then dig down to about 60 cm and take another small sample.
3. Notice the differences between topsoil and subsoil. Pack the samples into six plastic bags. Seal and number the bags. Record the depth, texture, and moisture of the soil in each plastic bag in the Data Table.
4. In the classroom, carefully examine the soil. Use the sieve over the tray or white paper to separate organisms. Record the number of each type of organism you find. Place each organism in a glass jar. Be sure to add a small amount of the soil in which the organism was found. Observe the organisms carefully over the next few days.

5. Make several slides of soil samples for observation under a microscope. Each time you place small bits of soil on a glass slide, use the medicine dropper to add a drop of water to the sample. Cover the slide with a coverslip. Look under the microscope for protists, algae, and bacteria.
6. Place soil samples from different depths on the plastic plates. Moisten the samples with water. Place some by the window. Observe the samples for several days.
7. Place sand in one cup, topsoil in another cup, and subsoil in a third cup. Label the cups appropriately. Plant 10 radish seeds in each cup. Be sure to spread the seeds apart and to lightly water the soil. Observe the cups for several days.

Observations

DATA TABLE

Bag Number	Depth	Texture	Moistness	Organisms Observed
1				
2				
3				
4				
5				
6				

1. How many centimeters thick was the layer of topsoil?

____

2. How did the texture of the soil at the surface differ from the texture at 60 cm?

____

3. How many kinds of living things did you find in the topsoil?

____

4. What does each living thing use for food? ______________________

____

5. How many kinds of living things did you find 60 cm deep?

____

6. Describe living things that appeared on the plates after about a week.

____

Name ______________________ Class ____________ Date ________

Analysis and Conclusions

1. Did you find more organisms living closer to the surface or deeper in the soil? How can you explain this observation? ______________________

____

____

____

2. Did the radishes grow better in topsoil or in subsoil? How can you explain this observation? ______________________

____

____

____

____

3. When the topsoil erodes from a field, what would you expect to grow in the field?

____

____

____

Critical Thinking and Application

1. Why are living organisms important in maintaining fertile topsoil?

____

____

____

____

2. In addition to the organisms you found in this investigation, list three other organisms that live in the soil. ______________________

____

____

____

3. Lumber companies will now replant forest areas after cutting down the trees originally found there. How does this help reduce the problem of soil erosion?

4. Many people who live directly on the coast have their homes built up on stilts that are deeply buried in the sand. Is there a practical reason for this? Explain your answer.

Going Further

A soil's particular chemistry determines what type of vegetation will grow in it. For example, a soil can limit vegetation growth if it is too acidic or basic. Test a sample of the topsoil and subsoil you collected with a few drops of 2% litmus solution in order to determine your soil's pH.

Using a Stream Table

Background Information

A very effective device for examining erosion, deposition, and transportation of sediments is a stream table. You can make a stream table using a flat wooden, or molded plastic, seed tray from a nursery or by making your own.

To make a stream table, use a piece of thin plywood, 100 cm × 65 cm × 2 cm. Nail small pieces of wood, 10 cm × 2.5 cm, around the plywood base. Make a small opening at one end of the stream table and insert a piece of rubber tubing. This will allow water to drain into a catch bucket. Waterproof the stream table by caulking around the base and sides or use a plastic trash bag to line the inside. You can run a hose from a sink or use a siphon from a pail as a source of water. The hose should have a spray nozzle. A watering can can also be used to simulate "rainfall."

In this investigation you will use a stream table to investigate running water and erosion. You will notice stream wandering, undercutting, deltas, deposits, and other features.

Problem

How can a stream table be used to investigate the effects of running water on the land?

Materials *(per class)*

stream table
sand
gravel
wooden block, 4 cm × 10 cm
buckets
hose with spray nozzle or a sprinkling can

Procedure

1. Obtain a moist mixture of sand and gravel that is sufficient to cover the bottom of the stream table to a depth of about 1.5–2.0 cm. Place the mixture in the stream table, leaving an area at the bottom empty. You can create some surface features such as hills, valleys, and so on. Using a wooden block, raise one end of the stream table slightly. See Figure 1.
2. At the raised end of the table, lightly spray the surface from a water source, such as a sprinkling can or hose with a spray nozzle connected to the sink. This water source represents "rainfall." Observe the stream patterns that develop. Draw an aerial view of the stream pattern in the space provided in Observations.

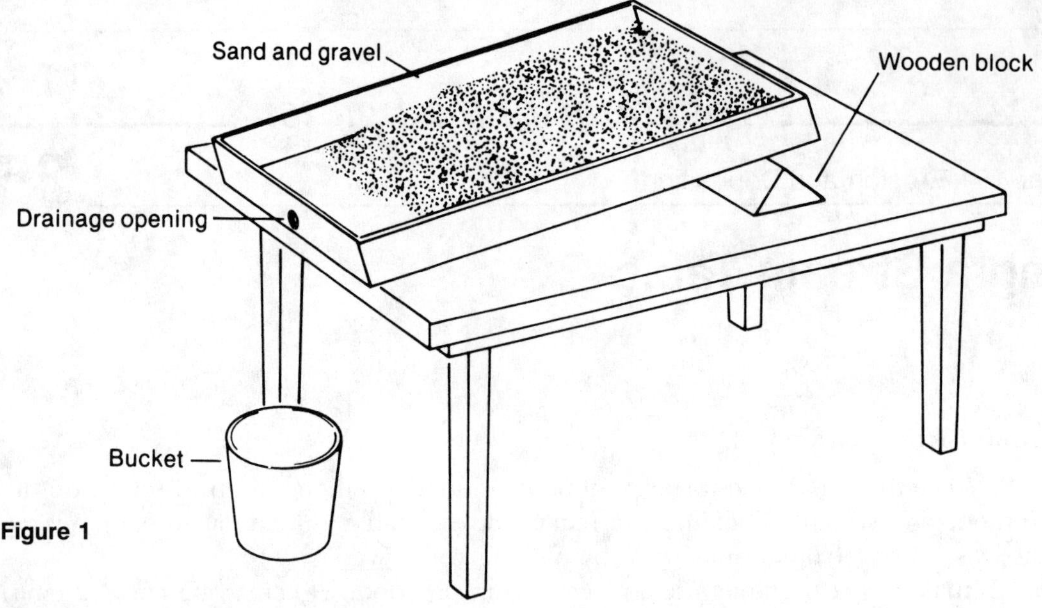

Figure 1

3. After the water has drained out, draw the material that has been carried down the "stream" and deposited at the mouth of the stream in the space provided in Observations. Be sure to note where the large pebbles have been carried and where the small sand grains have been deposited.

4. Arrange the sand and gravel in the stream table as in step 1. This time raise the stream table at one end to double the height.

5. Lightly spray the water as in step 2. Once again draw the aerial view of the "stream" and an aerial view of the "delta" and deposited materials in the space provided in Observations.

6. Draw a small part of the "stream" along a straight section and along a curved section in the spaces provided in Observations.

Observations

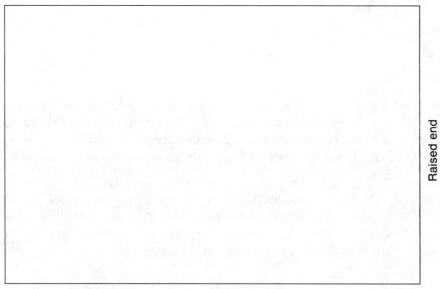

Aerial View of Stream Pattern

Name ____________________ Class __________ Date ________

Raised end

Aerial View of Delta and Deposited Material

Raised end

Aerial View of Stream Pattern and Delta (Slope Increased)

Straight Section of Stream

Curved Section of Stream

Analysis and Conclusions

1. What effect does the steepness of the slope have on the stream pattern?

2. What effect does the steepness of the slope have on the amount of material carried by the stream?

3. If a dam were placed across the "stream," what would you notice?

4. What difference do you notice between the sections of the stream that are straight and those that are curved?

Critical Thinking and Application

1. Old rivers have a tendency to meander. Explain why this happens.

2. How do you think ground cover, such as trees or grass, would affect the rate of erosion produced by a stream?

3. Why do streams carry more soil and rock material during a flood than during regular times? ________________

4. If the rainfall were the same in both areas, do you think runoff would be greater in a warmer climate or a cooler climate? Explain your answer.

5. Would you classify the Colorado River, which runs through the Grand Canyon, as an old or a young river? On what evidence would you base your answer?

Going Further

Use the stream table to investigate the effects of a melting glacier. Mix 1 L of sand and gravel with 500 mL of clay and water in a cake pan. Freeze the mixture until solid. Remove the pan from the freezer and place it on the raised portion of the stream table. Write a report explaining what happens as the "glacier" melts.

Observing Sediment Deposition in Quiet Water

Background Information

As flowing streams and rivers empty into ponds and lakes, they carry with them bits and pieces of rock and soil. These small particles are known as sediment. Sediment begins when the processes of weathering act on the materials that make up the Earth's crust.

When the waters that carry sediment flow into a body of quiet water, such as a lake, various things can happen to the particles that make up the sediment. Some of them settle to the bottom of the lake almost immediately; others take much longer. Some particles may take years to settle out. Still others become dissolved in the lake water and never sink to the bottom.

In this investigation you will construct a model body of water and observe how sediment is deposited on the bottom.

Problem

How do differences in size and density of particles affect the length of time it takes for the particles to settle in quiet water?

Materials *(per group)*

3 plastic columns
3 rubber stoppers for columns
timer
ring stand
2 burette clamps
sand particles of different sizes
equal-sized particles of different density

Procedure

Part A Particle Size and Settling Time

1. Insert a rubber stopper into a plastic column. Use the clamps to set up the apparatus as shown in Figure 1. Add water to the plastic column until it is about three-quarters full.

2. Examine the sand particles of different sizes. Record the relative sizes of the particles, from largest to smallest, in Data Table 1.

3. Drop a pinch of the largest sand particles into the column. Record the time it takes for most of the particles to reach the bottom in Data Table 1. Disregard any particles that float on the surface. Drop a second pinch of large sand particles and again record the time they take to reach the bottom in Data Table 1.

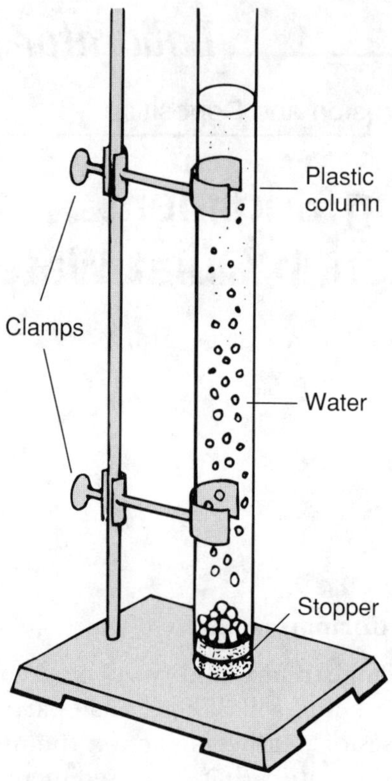

Figure 1

4. Repeat this procedure for each size sand particle. Calculate the average settling time for each particle size. Record it in the proper space in Data Table 1.

Part B Particle Density and Settling Time

1. Remove the plastic column and set it aside. Attach another plastic column fitted with a rubber stopper. Fill the column three-quarters full with water.

2. Gather equal-sized particles of different density. Glass beads and BBs have been provided. Record their relative density, from higher to lower, in Data Table 2.

3. Determine the settling time for the different particles. To do this, determine the settling time for one sample of each density and then repeat the procedure. Record these results in Data Table 2.

4. Calculate the average settling time for samples of each different density and record your results in Data Table 2.

Name ______________________ Class ____________ Date ________

Part C Settling Pattern of Mixed Particles

1. Remove the plastic container and set it aside. Insert another plastic container fitted with a rubber stopper into the apparatus and fill it three-quarters full with water.
2. Drop a handful of sand particles of different sizes into the column. Let them settle to the bottom.
3. Carefully observe the nature and extent of the sorting out of particles as they collect on the bottom of the column. In Figure 2 of Observations, sketch what you see in detail.

Observations

DATA TABLE 1

Relative Particle Size	Trial 1	Trial 2	Average Time
Largest			

DATA TABLE 2

Particle Type	Relative Density	Trial 1	Trial 2	Average Density

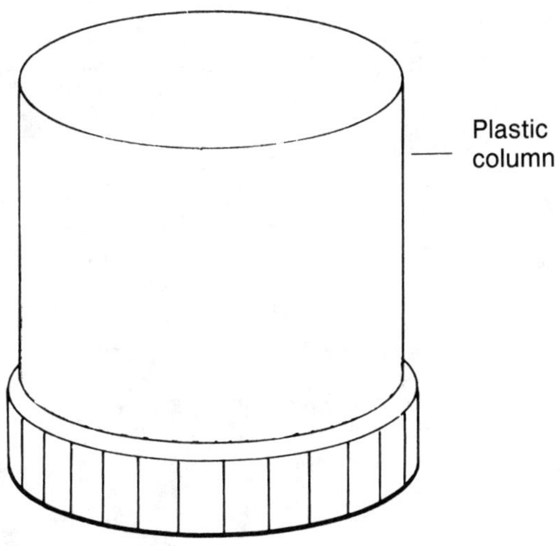

Figure 2

Analysis and Conclusions

1. What effect does size have on the length of time it takes for particles of sediment to settle in quiet water? ____

2. What effect does density have on the length of time it takes for particles of sediment to settle in quiet water? ____

Critical Thinking and Application

1. If particles of different sizes are dropped into quiet water, describe the order in which they would settle. ____

2. An observer reported that she found large particles of sand deposited on top of smaller particles in a sample of sediment. Give a possible explanation for her discovery.

Going Further

Devise an experiment to determine the effect of size and density on particle deposition in running water. Perform the experiment. How do your results compare to the results of this investigation?

Laboratory Investigation

Constructing a Barometer for Observing Changes in Air Pressure

Background Information

As the temperature and moisture content of the Earth's atmosphere vary, the variation causes changes in atmospheric density. Whenever the density of the atmosphere changes, the force that it exerts at the Earth's surface changes also. Such variations result in pressure differences, which are responsible in large part for the type of weather in a given location. As a result, "weather watchers" are often interested in knowing whether air pressure is changing. People have developed instruments that are able to detect even the slightest changes in atmospheric pressure. Such instruments are known as barometers.

In this investigation you will construct a simple barometer and use it to make observations of changes in atmospheric pressure.

Problem

How can a simple instrument be constructed that will detect pressure differences due to the changes in the weight of the air?

Materials *(per group)*

wide-mouthed container such as a coffee can
medium to large rubber balloon
piece of broom straw 12 to 15 cm long
glue
1 sheet of unlined paper
pencil
metric ruler
scissors
rubber band

Procedure

1. Check the open top of the container to be certain it has no rough or sharp edges.

2. Briefly inflate and then deflate the balloon. Cut off the neck of the balloon as shown in Figure 1.

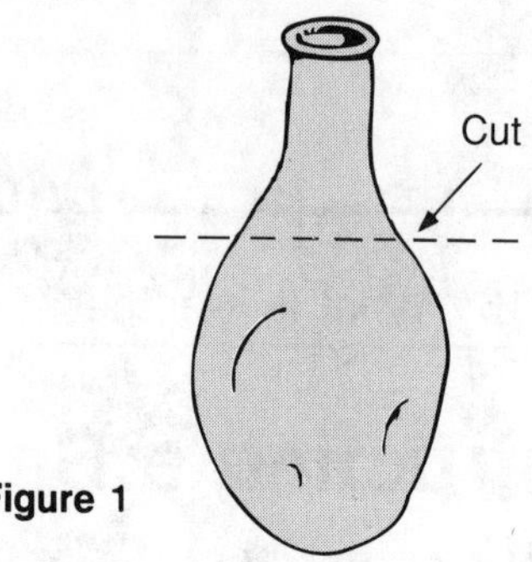

Figure 1

3. Fold the cut edges of the balloon outward and carefully stretch the balloon over the open end of the container. See Figure 2. Take care that the balloon does not rip or tear. A rubber band can be used to hold the balloon more tightly to the rim of the coffee can.

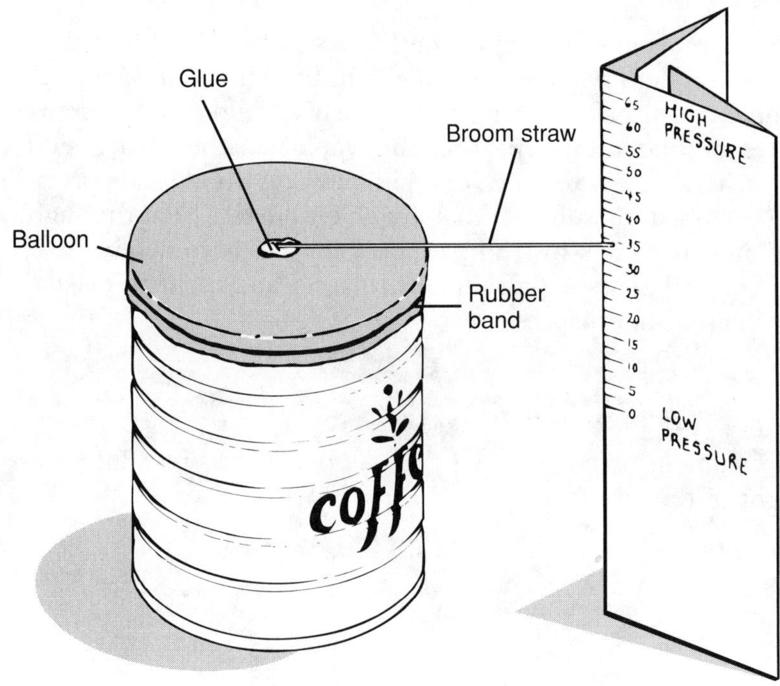

Figure 2

4. Place a small amount of glue on the center of the rubber balloon top.

5. Attach one end of the broom straw to the glue while allowing the remaining portion to simply rest upon the rim of the container. **Note:** *Do not attach the straw at the rim.* It should extend several centimeters beyond the edge of the container. See Figure 2.

6. While the glue is setting, fold the unlined sheet of paper as shown in Figure 2. Using the ruler, draw a scale along the central folded edge. The marks should be 0.5 cm apart. Write "High pressure" at the top of your scale and "Low pressure" at the bottom.

7. After the straw has been firmly attached to the top of your barometer, place the barometer and the paper scale in a location that is as free from temperature changes as possible. Arrange the scale and the barometer as shown in Figure 2.

8. Observe and record any changes in air pressure that are indicated by your barometer during a period of at least one week. Also record the general weather conditions present on those days. Record your observations in the Data Table.

Name ______________________ Class __________ Date __________

Observations

DATA TABLE

	Air Pressure	General Weather Conditions
Day 1		
Day 2		
Day 3		
Day 4		
Day 5		

Analysis and Conclusions

1. What change in the atmosphere must occur in order for the free end of the broom straw to rise? ______________________

2. What change must occur in order for it to fall?

3. According to your observations, what kind of weather is usually associated with high air pressure? ______________________

Critical Thinking and Application

1. What would happen to the operation of your barometer if the balloon were to develop a tiny opening? ______________________

2. What, if any, effect would a great temperature change have on the accuracy of your barometer? ____________________

____

____

3. The air pressure inside a tornado is extremely low. How might a barometer be used to detect the approach of a tornado? ____________________

____

____

____

4. In addition to a barometer, what other devices provide weather information?

____

____

____

Going Further

Compare the changes in air pressure indicated by your barometer to air pressure changes shown on weather maps published in a local newspaper during the same time period. Do they agree? If not, explain why you think they were not the same.

Laboratory Investigation

Investigating Weather Maps

Background Information

Weather forecasting is made possible through the analysis of detailed information that describes atmospheric conditions from several locations. In the United States, weather data from more than 300 local weather stations are used to prepare daily weather maps that present an overall picture of the weather throughout the country for a particular time. A detailed map may contain more than 10,000 items of weather data. Such a map will become the basis for making weather predictions.

In this investigation you will prepare a simplified weather map from limited data. Then you will analyze the map to discover relationships between atmospheric variables.

Problem

How are weather maps prepared? How can weather maps be used to better understand relationships between atmospheric variables?

Materials *(per group)*

pencil
colored pencils or crayons

Procedure

Part A Information From Observation Stations

1. Figure 1 illustrates the correct placement of some weather data recorded at an observation station. You will plot similar data on a map of the United States.

2. The circle in Figure 1 represents the observation station. Weather data are placed in specific positions inside and outside the circle.

Station Circle

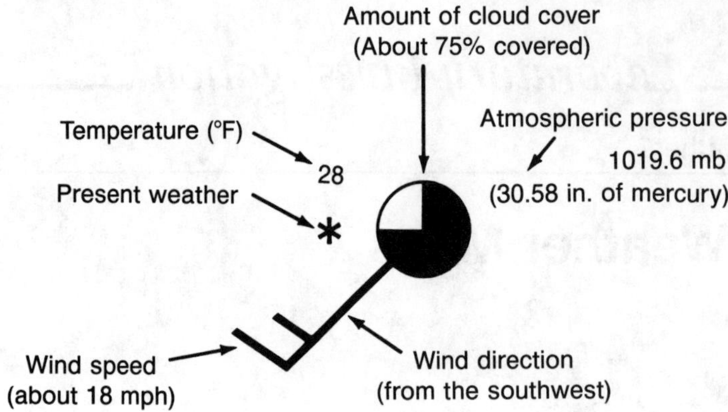

Figure 1

3. *Wind direction:* You should think of the station circle as the point of an arrow. Attached to the station circle is a line, which is the arrow's shaft. The wind direction is represented as moving along the arrow's shaft *toward* the center of the station circle. Wind directions are given in degrees and represent the direction *from which* the wind is blowing. In Figure 1, the wind is blowing from the southwest toward the northeast. Figure 2 will help you determine wind direction.

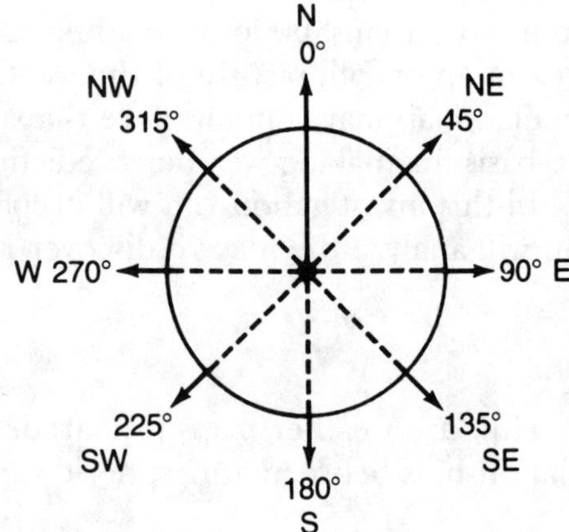

Figure 2

4. *Wind speed:* Often there are small lines that resemble arrow feathers at the end of the shaft. These lines are symbols for wind speed. Each full line represents an increase in speed of about 10 miles per hour. Half a line is about 5 miles per hour. If there is only one "feather," place it at the end of the arrow if it is a full feather, and slightly farther in if it is a half feather. Although the metric unit of speed is kilometers per hour, miles per hour has been used in this investigation because it is the unit most commonly found on weather maps.

5. *Atmospheric pressure:* Look at a weather map in your local newspaper. You will see long, curving lines that have a number attached to them. These lines are called isobars. Some of the curves are closed; some, open. Isobars are lines joining places on a weather map that have the same atmospheric pressure. The numbers associated with these lines are the atmospheric pressure recorded at each observation station. These pressures are measured in millibars. So isobars are measured in millibars. Look at the column of atmospheric pressures in Figure 6. To determine the pressure in millibars, use only the last three digits of the pressures listed and omit the decimal point. An example (196) is given in Figure 1.

6. *Temperature:* The average daily temperature is usually recorded in degrees Fahrenheit.
7. *Present weather:* From the list in Figure 3, select the symbol that most accurately describes the weather existing at each observation station listed in Figure 6 when the data were collected.
8. *Cloud coverage:* Using Figure 4, indicate the amount of cloud cover at each observation station. This information is enclosed within each circle. Put this information in the circles on the map in Figure 7.
9. Now transfer all the weather information listed in Figure 6 to the specific observation stations shown in Figure 7.

Weather Symbols

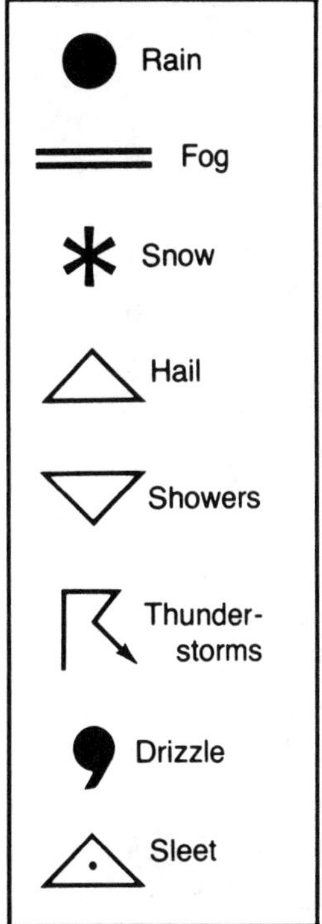

Figure 3

Cloud Cover

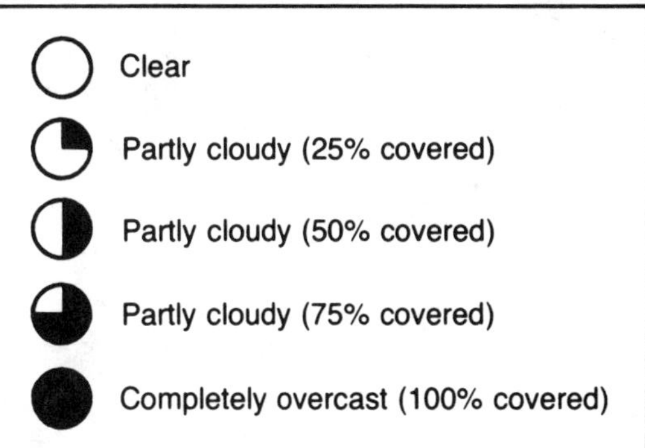

Figure 4

Fronts

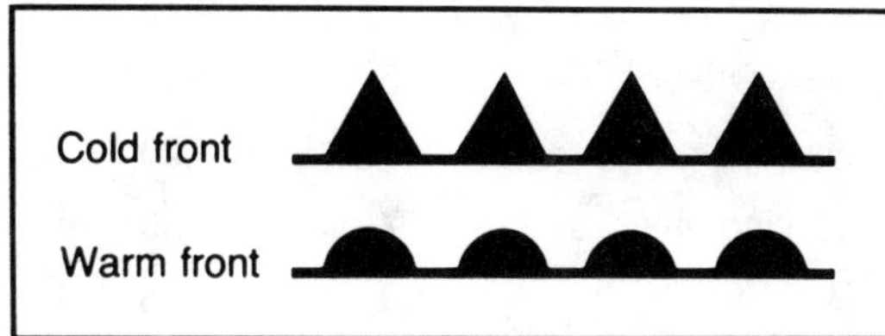

Figure 5

Part B Additional Weather Map Information

1. In Figure 7, locate the observation station with the lowest atmospheric pressure and write the word "Low" just above it. Starting at this point, which is the center of a low-pressure area, draw in the cold and warm fronts. The symbols are shown in Figure 5.

The cold front comes out of the high-pressure center. This front, when placed in Figure 7, will be located between stations where winds change from southwest to northwest and temperatures decrease suddenly. The warm front comes out of the low-pressure center. This front, when placed in Figure 7, will be located between stations where winds change from east to southeast and temperatures rise suddenly.

OBSERVATION STATIONS

Weather Station	Wind Speed (mph)	Wind Direction	Atmospheric Pressure (mb)	Temperature (°F)	Type of Precipitation	Cloud Cover (%)
Seattle	7	260°	1020.8	42		0
Bend	10	200°	1023.5	40		0
San Francisco	8	135°	1020.0	48	Fog	25
Los Angeles	0		1021.1	41	Fog	25
Phoenix	11	50°	1021.1	45		0
Ely	0		1025.1	37		0
Dubois	18	225°	1024.0	38		0
Helena	15	315°	1020.0	41		0
Medicine Hat	20	345°	1020.1	40		0
Bismarck	18	0°	1014.3	48		0
Casper	12	350°	1016.0	50		0
Pueblo	8	315°	1015.3	47		0
Roswell	22	350°	1016.0	48		0
Del Rio	38	315°	1012.0	50	Thunderstorms	100
Galveston	5	225°	1016.0	72		25
Dallas	29	315°	1007.9	60	Hail	100
Oklahoma City	45	315°	1007.7	57	Thunderstorms	100
Kansas City	0		1002.3	58	Rain	100
Burwell	22	325°	1009.3	52	Rain	100
Minneapolis	15	45°	1008.2	51	Drizzle	100
Sioux Lookout	20	50°	1016.8	46		25
Chicago	10	45°	1005.2	58	Drizzle	100
Little Rock	8	225°	1009.3	67		25
New Orleans	5	225°	1017.9	73		0
Nashville	5	220°	1011.1	68		25
Cincinnati	7	90°	1009.8	57	Rain	100
Detroit	10	75°	1011.9	54	Drizzle	100
Sault Ste. Marie	15	45°	1013.1	50	Drizzle	100
Ert	5	100°	1017.2	48		0
Quebec	0		1017.0	50		25
Boston	12	100°	1018.1	52	Fog	25
Buffalo	7	75°	1016.0	52	Drizzle	100
New York	10	80°	1017.6	56	Fog	50
Hatteras	14	90°	1019.1	60		50
Charleston	15	225°	1017.8	70		25
Atlanta	3	225°	1014.6	70		0
Jacksonville	2	200°	1018.1	73		0
Tampa	2	230°	1018.0	74		25
Miami	0		1019.8	78		0

Figure 6

Name ______________________ Class __________ Date __________

2. Locate the observation station in Figure 7 with the highest atmospheric pressure and write the word "High" just above it. This is the center of an area of high pressure.

3. Draw the following isobars in Figure 7: 1004 mb, 1008 mb, 1012 mb, 1016 mb, 1020 mb, and 1024 mb. Draw these isobars so that they point away from the center of the low-pressure area when they cross cold or warm fronts. Label each isobar. Remember that isobars are long, curving lines. They connect locations on a weather map that have the same atmospheric pressure. It will be helpful to review the atmospheric pressures listed in Figure 6.

4. In Figure 7, draw a line around all the locations where precipitation has fallen. Either use a pencil and shade in the area with precipitation or use a colored pencil or crayon and color in this area.

Observations

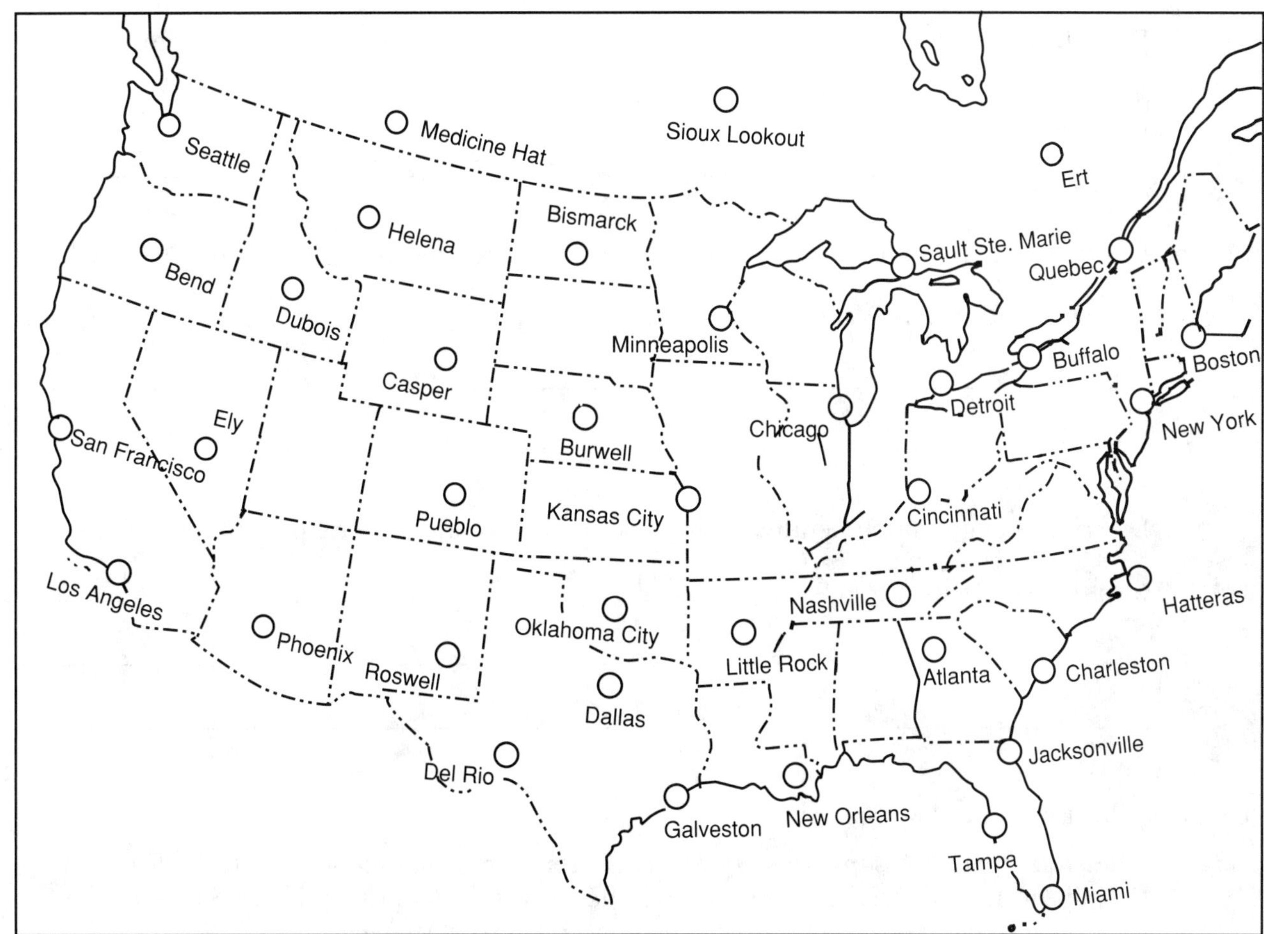

Figure 7

Analysis and Conclusions

1. An area of high pressure is referred to as an anticyclone, and an area of low pressure is called a cyclone. According to your weather map, is precipitation generally associated with a cyclone or an anticyclone? ______

2. Compare wind direction of air around a low-pressure center with wind direction around a high-pressure center. ______

3. Compare the type of precipitation associated with the cold front to that associated with the warm front. ______

4. Describe the location of the precipitation associated with the warm front as compared to the precipitation associated with the cold front. ______

5. Describe changes in temperature, wind direction, and atmospheric pressure associated with the passage of a warm front. ______

6. Describe changes in temperature, wind direction, and atmospheric pressure associated with the passage of a cold front. ______

Critical Thinking and Application

1. Refer to Figure 7. Assume that the storm center is moving in a northeasterly direction. Describe at least three changes in the weather in Cincinnati, Ohio, if the center of the low-pressure area becomes located directly over Detroit, Michigan.

______

Name ______________________ Class ____________ Date ________

2. Identify the error in each of the following observation station reports.

a.

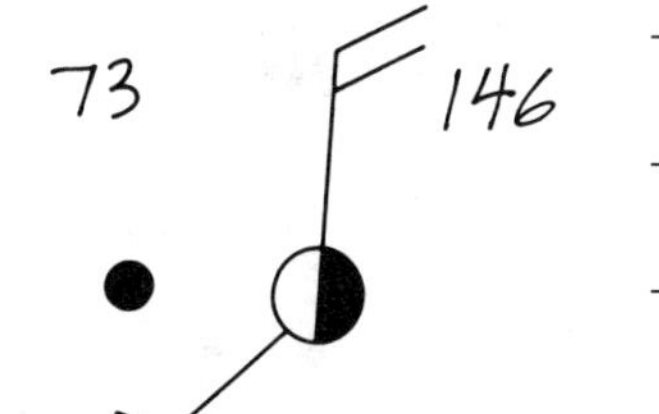

____

____

____

b.

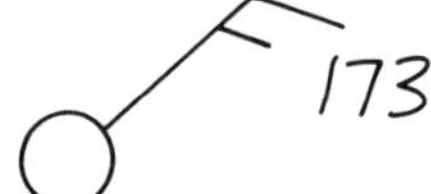

____

____

____

c.

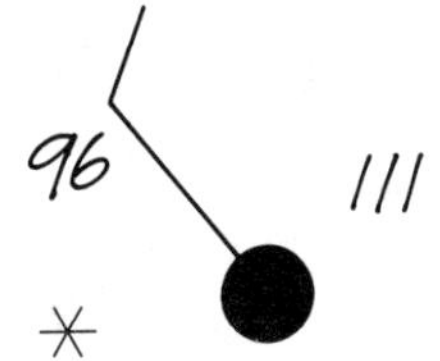

____

____

____

3. Is it possible for yesterday's weather map to help you to predict tomorrow's weather?

Explain your answer. ____

____

____

____

Going Further

1. Wind speed is normally given in miles per hour on a weather map. Change all the wind speeds listed in Figure 6 to kilometers per hour.
2. There are four major types of air masses that affect the weather in the United States. Each of them brings different weather conditions. Look up information in the library about these air masses. Then label the areas on your weather map behind the cold front, in front of the cold front, and in front of the warm front with the appropriate air mass symbol. The names and symbols for these air masses are continental polar (cP), continental tropical (cT), maritime tropical (mT), and maritime polar (mP).

Name ______________________ Class ____________ Date ________

Laboratory Investigation

Chapter 17 What Is Climate? **39**

Investigating Differences in Climate

Background Information

You have learned that there are many different types of climates. You have also learned that many factors are responsible for such climatic differences. However, each of these factors can eventually be reduced to two major categories: those that affect the average yearly temperature of an area and those that affect the average yearly precipitation.

In this investigation you will study the effect of the relationship between available energy and moisture on the climate of various regions. The amount of available energy helps to determine the temperature of a region. For this investigation you will use the ratio of average yearly precipitation *(P)* to average yearly potential evapotranspiration (E_p). These climate ratios, written as P/E_p, represent the average yearly moisture supply divided by the moisture demand, or need, at a certain location. The word evapotranspiration refers to the total water loss from the soil, including direct evaporation, and transpiration, which is the giving off of moisture through the surface of leaves and other plant parts.

Four different climatic types based on P/E_p values are generally recognized: arid, semiarid, subhumid, and humid. Each different type and its climate ratios are given in Figure 1.

P/E_p	Climate Type
Less than 0.4	Arid
0.4–0.8	Semiarid
0.8–1.2	Subhumid
Greater than 1.2	Humid

Figure 1

Problem

What climate patterns of an imaginary continent can be drawn when you draw lines to connect similar climate ratios? What is the location of different climate types of an imaginary continent when you are given precipitation *(P)* and potential evapotranspiration (E_p) data?

Materials *(per group)*

map of the imaginary continent of Ert
soft graphite pencil
colored pencils or crayons

Procedure

1. Carefully examine Figure 2, a map of an imaginary continent. The numbers at various locations are the climate ratios for those areas. Notice that the continent of Ert is a very large continent, extending poleward beyond latitudes 60° north and south. Notice also that there is a very extensive mountain range along the west coast, as well as two separate mountain ranges along the east coast.

2. The following information is important to remember when working on your map:

   a. Climate ratios greater than 1.2 are usually found in regions at or near the equator. These regions are generally humid.

   b. Regions at or near latitudes 30° north and south are generally arid, unless influenced by mountain ranges or other factors. Climate ratios of 0.4 or less are usually found in these regions.

   c. Areas at or near latitudes 60° north and south are generally moist but have climate ratios that often show wide variations because of the influence of global wind systems, large bodies of water, and mountain ranges.

   d. When drawing climate ratio lines, remember that the lines of any climate type cannot cross. They tend to run parallel to each other and do not form sharp edges or acute angles. Also, these lines must be continuous; that is, they must form closed loops or run off the edges of the continent.

3. Try to locate the regions on the imaginary continent that are most arid and humid. Find the locations of mountain ranges and specific lines of latitude.

4. Using a soft graphite pencil, lightly connect each location with a 0.4 climate ratio. Notice that there are two separate regions having such a climate ratio, one in each hemisphere. The 0.4 line located in the Southern Hemisphere has been sketched in for you as an example of a correctly drawn climate ratio.

5. Lightly draw in lines that have a 0.8 climate ratio.

6. Draw in lines connecting regions that have 0.0, 1.2, and 1.6 climate ratios.

7. Upon completion of your map, darken the lines and identify the areas between the lines as arid, semiarid, humid, or subhumid. For example, regions located between climate lines 0.4 and 0.8 should be labeled semiarid. Regions between 0.8 and 1.2 should be labeled subhumid. Color the different regions on your map. Be sure to include a color key identifying these regions.

Name ______________________ Class ____________ Date ________

Observations

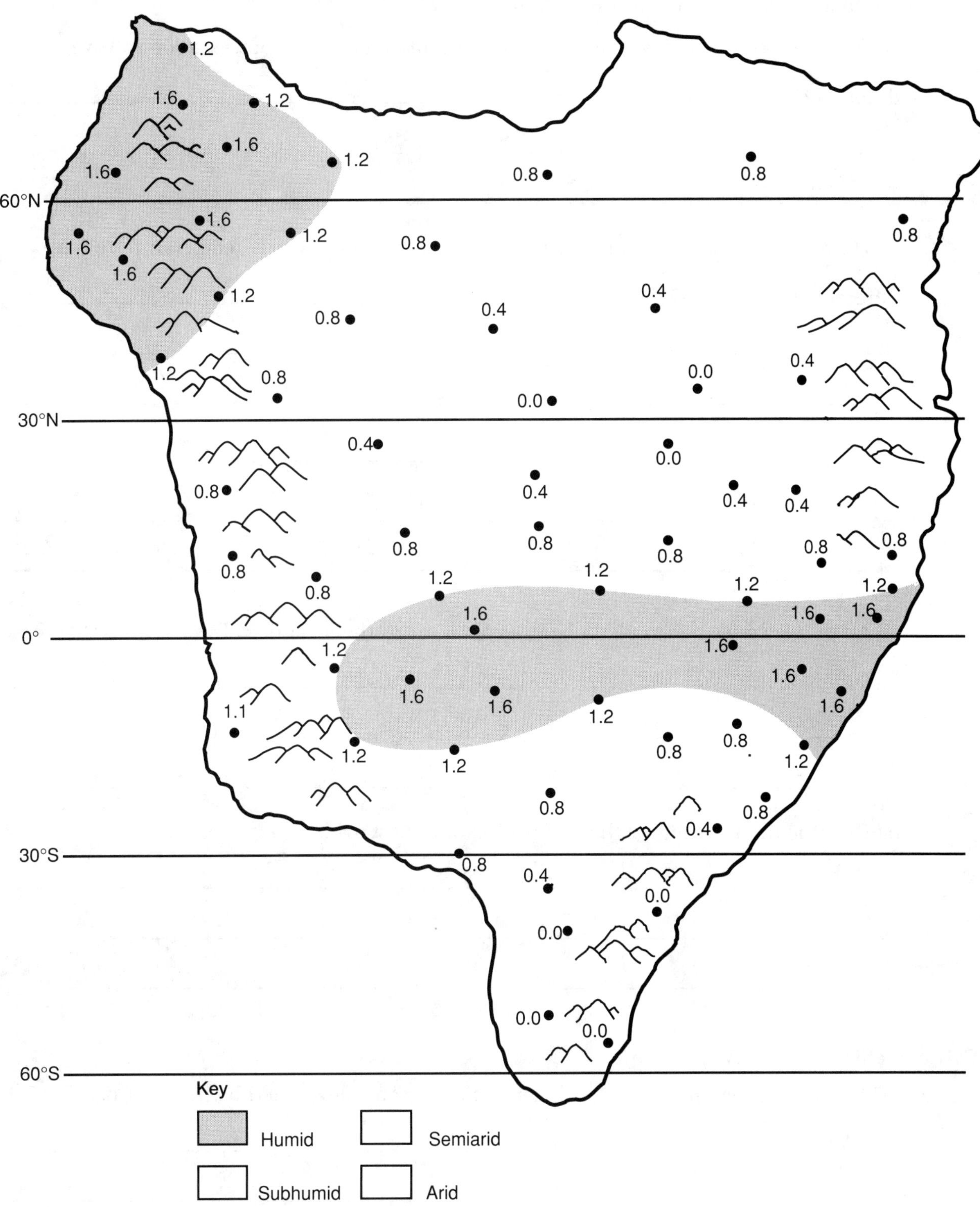

Figure 2

Analysis and Conclusions

1. You have learned that the climate ratio (P/E_p) is actually a comparison of a region's precipitation (P) to its potential evapotranspiration (E_p). You have also learned that the potential evapotranspiration value is directly related to a region's temperature: the higher the temperature, the higher the E_p value.

   a. How is it possible for two regions with the same total yearly precipitation to have different climate ratios? ____________________

   b. How is it possible for two regions with the same average yearly temperature to have different climate ratios? ____________________

2. What relationship exists between latitude and temperature patterns?

3. a. According to your map, describe in general terms the locations of the regions that are most humid. ____________________

   b. Describe the locations of the regions that are most arid.

Critical Thinking and Application

1. What areas on the imaginary continent of Ert do you think would be the most heavily populated? Explain your answer. ____________________

2. In which of the four climatic regions do you think you live? On what evidence do you base your answer? ______

3. How does the climate of your area affect each of the following: the type of clothing that is worn; the type of plants or animals that are raised for food; the type of recreational activities that are enjoyed; energy consumption?

Going Further

Suppose the imaginary continent of Ert is located on the Earth. What reasons can you give to explain the locations of the most humid and most arid regions of Ert? Draw on your map the directions of the global winds from above 60°N to 60°S. See Figure 16–16 on page 499 in your textbook. Also label each latitude line shown on your map as an area of generally (1) high or low air pressure and (2) wet or dry weather conditions. Remember from Chapter 16 in your textbook that winds flow from high-pressure areas to low-pressure areas.

Since winds flow from high-pressure areas to low-pressure areas, humid climates are associated with (1) being close to large bodies of water that supply moisture brought inland by global winds, (2) low-pressure systems as winds tend to flow toward these regions, and (3) wet weather conditions. Arid climates are associated with (1) being far from large bodies of water, (2) high-pressure systems as winds tend to flow away from these regions, (3) moisture loss as air moves over barriers such as mountain ranges, and (4) dry weather conditions.

Name ______________________ Class __________ Date ________

Laboratory Investigation

Chapter 18 Climate in the United States **40**

Adaptations of Plants in Different Biomes

Background Information

The climate of a region determines the kinds of plants that can grow in any particular region. Climate, or average temperature and precipitation, is just one of the abiotic (nonliving) factors of the environment that determines what kinds of living things will live in an area. Other abiotic factors are sunlight, wind, and soil quality.

In this investigation you will explore how plants are adapted to the abiotic factors in their environment.

Problem

How are plants adapted for life in a particular biome?

Materials *(per class)*

lichen
conifer branch
deciduous leaves
bromeliad
buffalo grass
cactus
6 hand lenses

Procedure

1. Examine the lichen, noting its overall height. Use the hand lens to study its tiny rootlike structures.
2. Study the conifer branch. Observe the size and shape of its needlelike leaves. Notice that they are covered with a waxy outer covering called a cuticle.
3. Examine a deciduous leaf. Compare the deciduous leaf with a conifer needle.
4. Examine the bromeliad, which grows in tropical rain forests. Study the cuplike arrangement of the leaves.
5. Study the structure of the buffalo grass, using the hand lens to examine the root system.
6. Carefully examine the cactus. Study the thick, fleshy stem and the sharp spines, being careful not to hurt yourself. Locate and examine the root system.
7. Study the chart of the abiotic factors in biomes.

ABIOTIC FACTORS IN BIOMES

Biome	Annual Precipitation	Average Temperature	Growing Season	Soil	Other Seasonal Features
Tundra	Very dry, less than 25 cm	Ranges from below −30° to 10°C	Very short, less than 60 days	Few minerals; soil frozen except for top layer	Long, cold winters; short summers
Coniferous forest	Dry, 50 to 125 cm	Ranges from −30° to 20°C	Short, 60 to 150 days	Poor, acidic soil; nutrients lacking	Long, cold, snowy winters; warmer summers than tundra
Deciduous forest	Moderate, 75 to 150 cm	North, from −12° to 27°C; south, from 15° to 30°C	Moderate, 180 days or more	Good soil, with nutrients	Long, warm summers; north, cold winters; south, warmer winters
Grassland	Dry, 25 to 75 cm, with irregular precipitation patterns and drought	Wide temperature range between deciduous forest and desert	Moderate, 180 days or more	Very rich soil	Long, warm summers; winters severe in some areas
Tropical rain forest	Very wet, over 200 cm	Constant high temperatures; 24° to 26°C	Very long, all year	Poor soil; minerals and nutrients washed away by rain	Warm and humid all year
Desert	Very dry, less than 25 cm, with irregular precipitation patterns and drought	Cold desert, 10°C; hot desert, over 20°C	Depends on type of desert	Poor, sandy soil	Depends on type and location of desert

Observations

1. How are the rootlike structures of the lichen adapted for survival on the tundra?

____

____

____

2. How does the shape of a conifer's needles help adapt the tree for life in a coniferous forest? ____

____

____

3. How does the arrangement of leaves on a bromeliad help it to obtain moisture? ______

4. How do the stem and roots of the cactus help it to survive in the desert? ______

Analysis and Conclusions

1. Which absorbs sunlight better—a conifer needle or a deciduous leaf? Why? ______

2. Grasslands in the eastern part of the United States receive slightly more precipitation than those in the West. Where would you expect to find buffalo grass? Why? ______

Critical Thinking and Application

1. Which abiotic factor is mainly responsible for the formation of a desert? ______

2. Which biome would you expect to have the greatest variety of plants? Why? ______

Going Further

Make two terrariums: one to simulate a tropical rain forest biome and one to simulate a desert biome. Choose appropriate plants and abiotic conditions for each terrarium biome. **Note:** *Do not put animals into your terrarium biomes.*

Name ______________________ Class ____________ Date ________

Laboratory Investigation

Chapter 19 Earth's History in Fossils **41**

Interpreting Events From Fossil Evidence

Background Information

A fossil is any evidence of life in the prehistoric past. Fossils can be actual remains of animals, impressions, carbon residues, or tracks or trails left by a living organism. By using fossil records, scientists are able to piece together the story that fossils tell about the history of the Earth.

In this investigation you will use some present-day knowledge and common sense to interpret fossil evidence.

Problem

How can fossils relate the history of an era?

Materials *(per student)*

pencil

Procedure

1. Observe the diagram of the fossil footprints in Figure 1.

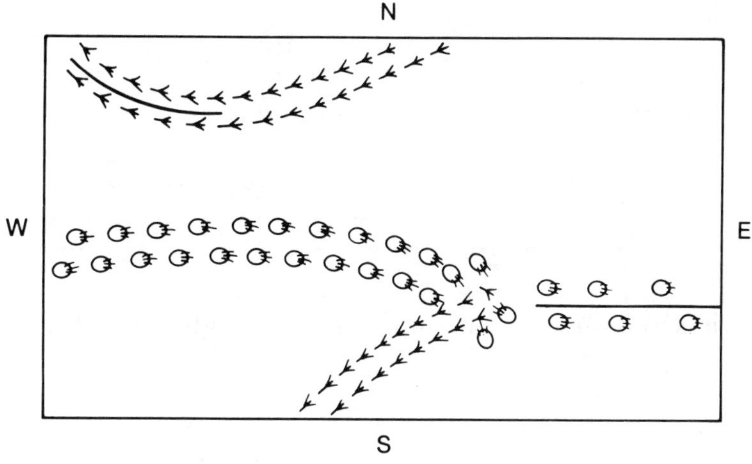

Figure 1

2. Answer the questions in Observations.
3. Using the answers to these questions and some common sense, interpret the events that may have occurred in Figure 1. **Note:** *Your interpretation should be consistent with the diagram.*

Observations

1. How would footprints be formed and preserved?

2. How can you tell in which direction the animal was walking?

3. How do footprints differ when an animal walks and when it runs?

4. a. Did the animals change speed? ___

   b. When? ___

5. How many different animals are represented?

6. How did the animals interact with one another?

Conclusions

1. Write a paragraph interpreting the footprints of the smaller animal in the upper left corner. Support your interpretations with evidence from the diagram.

2. Interpret the events in the lower right of the diagram.

3. If all the footprints were made within minutes of each other, which way was the wind blowing? Why? ___

4. In what kind of environment did this all take place?

Name ______ Class ______ Date ______

Critical Thinking and Application

1. In what type of rock would you be most likely to find fossils? Explain your answer.

2. Would you be likely to find the fossil remains of a jellyfish or a worm? Explain your answer.

3. The exposed rock layers of the Grand Canyon are rich with fossil specimens. What does the presence of fossil coral, sponges, shellfish, and trilobites indicate about the past environment of the Grand Canyon area? ______

4. How could our present-day environment be reconstructed 25,000 years from now, if all written history were to be lost or destroyed?

Going Further

Find out if there is a relationship between the depth of a footprint and the mass of a living thing. Have different people step in soft clay or soil. Measure the depth of the footprint and determine the relationship between the mass of a person and the depth of a footprint. Organize your information in a chart. Then interpret an "unknown" footprint.

Interpreting a Sediment Deposition Model

Background Information

Earth scientists often can interpret the rock in an area and describe how that area was formed. To do this, they use two basic laws.

1. Law of superposition: When sediments are deposited, the oldest sediments are deposited first, followed by the next oldest, and so on. The newest sediment is on the top.
2. Law of original horizontality: When sediments are deposited, they form beds that are essentially horizontal.

After these layers of sediments are turned into rock, several things can occur.

1. Layers can be raised and eroded.
2. Layers can be folded or faulted.
3. Layers can be divided by molten rock that rises from deep in the Earth, forming an intrusion.

By combining these ideas with careful observation, scientists are able to interpret events on the Earth's surface that may have happened thousands of years ago.

In this investigation you will create a model of sediment deposition. Using the laws of superposition and original horizontality, you will interpret the sequence of events that formed the model area.

Problem

How can you interpret the history of an area by examining rock layers?

Materials *(per group)*

2 small jars with covers
masking tape
spoon
sand
clay
gravel
pencil

Procedure

1. Using masking tape, label the first jar "A" and the second jar "B."
2. In jar A, place a spoonful of each of the following: sand, clay, and gravel. Add enough water to almost fill the jar. Cover the jar and shake it well.
3. Pour one half of the shaken mixture into jar B. Observe the sediments in jar A as they settle. After the sediments completely settle, draw and label the sediments.

4. Carefully place a pencil under one side of jar B without disturbing the sediments. Draw and label the sediments in jar B.

5. Once again, cover and shake the contents of jar A. Gently pour the entire contents into jar B as it rests on the pencil. **Note:** *Try not to disturb the original sediment layers.*

6. Allow the sediments to settle once again and draw and label the sediments.

Observations

Sediments After Settling—Jar A

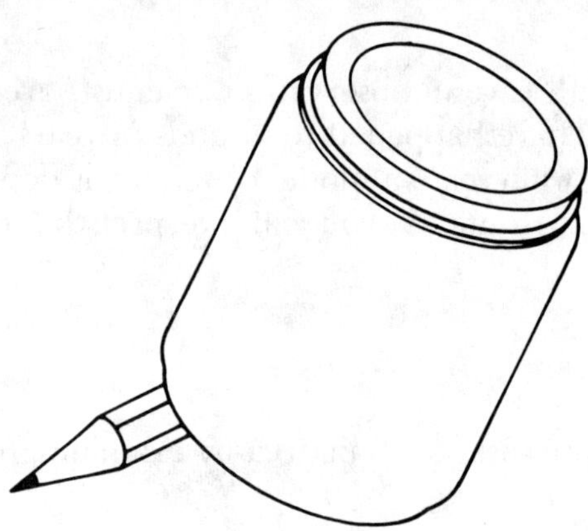

Sediment Layers—Jar B

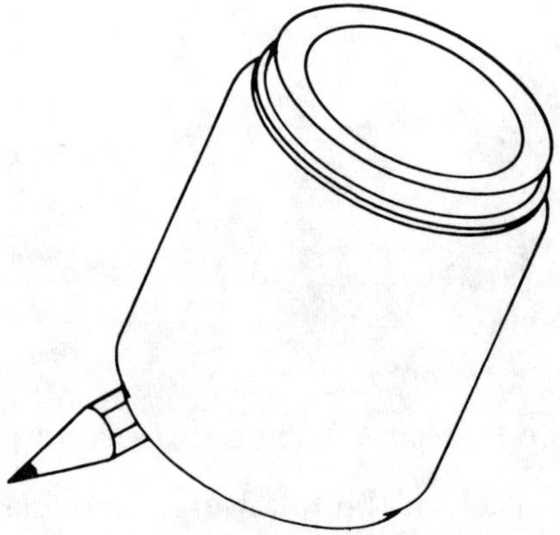

Sediment Layers—Jars A and B combined

Name ______________________ Class ____________ Date ________

Conclusions

1. What did you notice about the way the sediments were deposited in step 3? Explain your answer. ____

____

____

2. What did you notice about the way the new sediments settled in step 6?

____

____

____

3. If the pencil were removed and you were unaware of what happened, how could you tell the sequence of events that led to the final results?

____

____

____

____

4. How could you tell if a surface was uplifted and eroded, even if other sediments were later deposited on top? ____

____

____

5. Observe the following two cross sections. For each cross section, list the letters that correspond to the layers, intrusions, faults, and erosional surfaces in the order in which they were formed.

Cross Section 1

ORDER OF FORMATION

Cross Section 1

1st ______

2nd ______

3rd ______

4th ______

5th ______

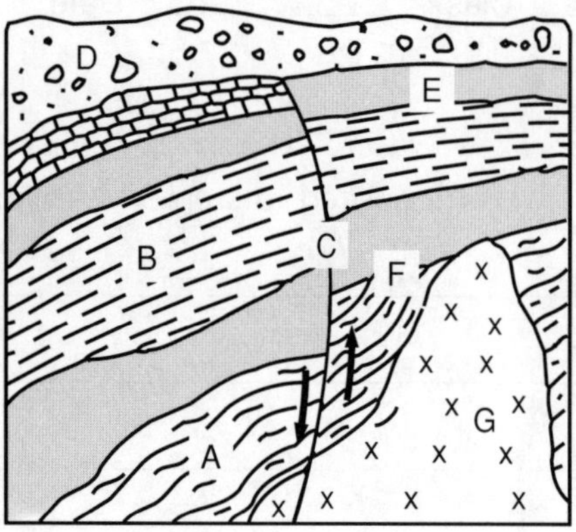

Cross Section 2

ORDER OF FORMATION

Cross Section 2

1st ______

2nd ______

3rd ______

4th ______

5th ______

6th ______

7th ______

Critical Thinking and Application

1. What factors can affect the rate of sedimentation that occurs in a river?

____

____

____

____

2. Is using the rate of sedimentation a good method of measuring the age of rock layers? Explain your answer. ____

____

____

3. Do you think dried lake or river beds would be good places to find fossils? Explain your answer. ____

____

____

____

4. How is the formation of a sand dune an exception to the law of original horizontality?

____

____

____

____

Going Further

1. Using a large, narrow jar, such as a liter juice jar, create a column of sediments by adding successive amounts of different sediments. You may want to use gravel, sand, soil, and clay. As you prepare the column, you may want to tilt the jar at various times. See if a classmate can interpret the sequence you used to create your sedimentary layers.
2. Using posterboard, crayons, paint, and colored pencils, create your own cross-section diagrams. Include intrusions and faults. See if a classmate can interpret the diagrams.

Laboratory Investigation

Using the Rock Record to Interpret Geologic History

Background Information

The North American continent has undergone major changes during its long history. It has been invaded by oceans, wracked by mountain formation, leveled by erosion, and scoured by glaciers. Many species of plants and animals appeared, flourished for a time, and then became extinct.

A detailed history can be told about our continent even though it occurred too long ago for us to have personally experienced it. Much of what is known has been gathered from long, careful investigations of the rock record.

In this investigation you will determine the age of rock layers and reconstruct the geologic history of an area from observations of subsurface rock layers.

Problem

What story does the rock record tell?

Materials *(per student)*

pencil

Procedure

1. The following general assumptions are used to determine the relative age of rock layers and reconstruct the geologic history of an area:
   a. In undisturbed sedimentary rock layers, the younger rock layers are on the top, and the layers get older as their depth below the surface increases.
   b. Igneous intrusions, rock faults, and rock folds are younger than the rock layers that are intruded into, faulted, or folded.
   c. Generally, either an area was below water and deposition of sediments took place, or it was above water and erosion took place.
2. Observe the following diagrams of subsurface rock layers. Then, using the three general assumptions, list the rock layers by number from the oldest to the youngest. Write the numbers on the lines next to each diagram. **Note:** *More than one number may appear on the same line, so all answer lines may not have to be used.*
3. Write a brief geologic history that explains the arrangement and relative positions of the rocks as shown in each diagram.

Observations

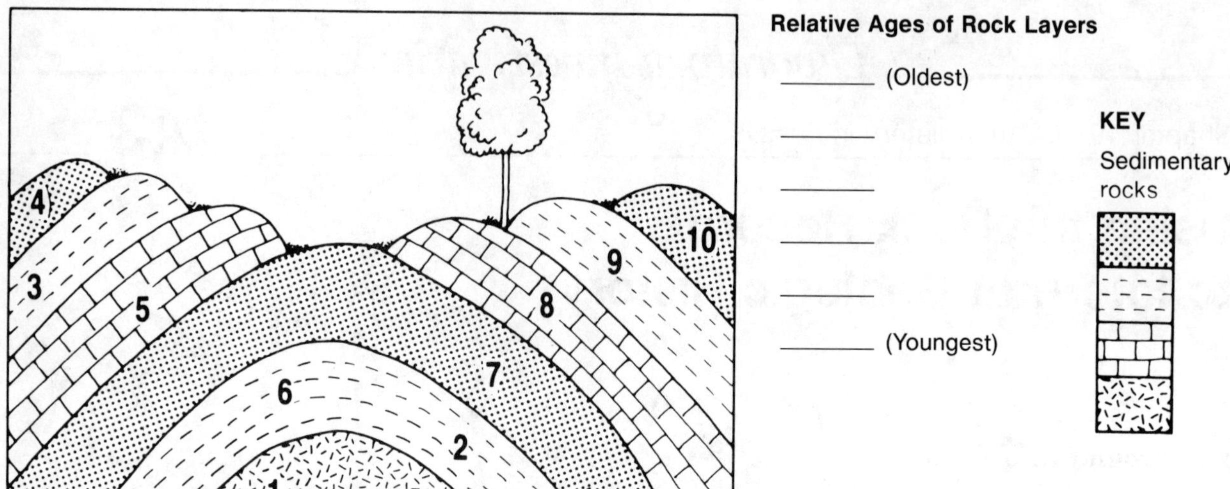

Figure 1

Geologic History:

____

____

____

____

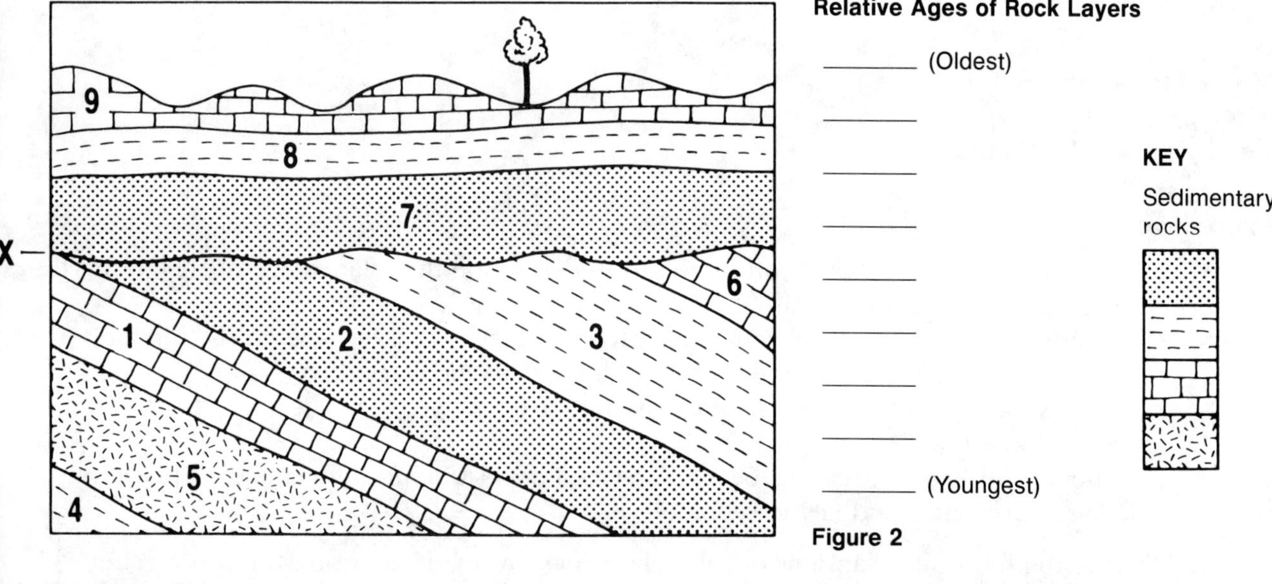

Figure 2

Geologic History:

____

____

____

____

____

Name ______________________ Class ______________ Date ____________

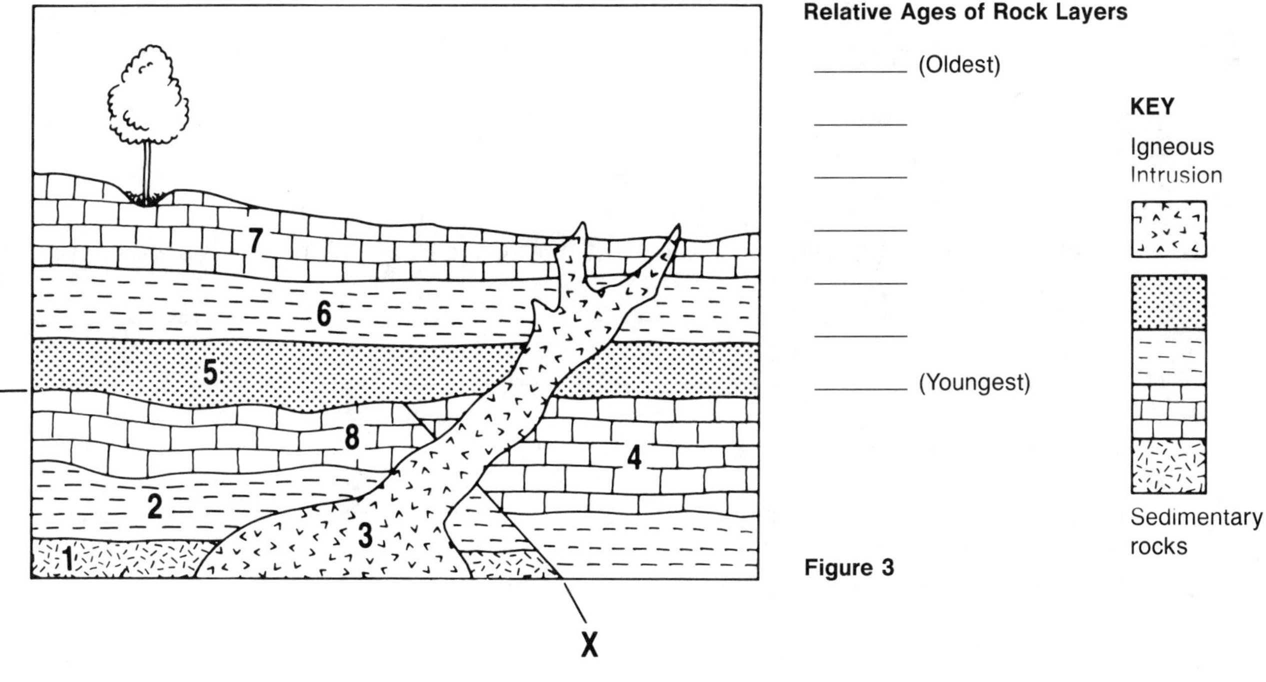

Relative Ages of Rock Layers

_______ (Oldest)

____

____

____

____

____

_______ (Youngest)

KEY

Igneous Intrusion

Sedimentary rocks

Figure 3

Geologic History:

____

____

____

____

____

Conclusions

Base your answers to questions 1 to 3 on the diagram below, which illustrates a cross section of subsurface rocks.

1. Which rock type is the youngest?

(a) A

(b) B

(c) C

(d) D

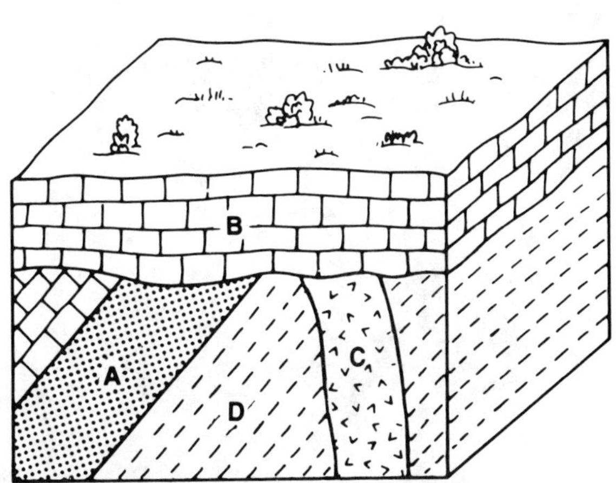

2. What was the last process to occur?

(a) The igneous intrusion of C

(b) The deposition of layer A

(c) The tilting of rock layers A and D

(d) The deposition of layer B

3. a. Which is the younger rock unit, C or D? ______________________________

b. Explain your answer. ______________________________

____

____

Critical Thinking and Application

1. Do you think there is any place on the Earth where the entire rock record is preserved in perfect form? Explain your answer. ______________________________

____

____

____

2. Why should a geologist use great caution in reconstructing the geologic history of an area that has many folds and faults? ______________________________

____

____

____

3. A paleontologist discovers a limestone rock layer that contains fossil remains of a bony fish. In a sandstone rock layer above this she discovers the fossils of a small, rodentlike mammal. What statement can the paleontologist make about the climate changes that have occurred over time? ______________________________

____

____

____

Going Further

Using a posterboard, crayons, paint, and colored pencils, create your own cross-section diagrams. Include intrusions and faults. See if a classmate can interpret the diagrams.

Laboratory Investigation

Demonstrating Half-Life

Background Information

The *half-life* of a radioactive element is the amount of time it takes for one half of the atoms in a sample of that element to decay, or break down into atoms of the stable decay element. Radioactive decay is one of the methods scientists use to measure geologic time and determine the absolute age of rocks and fossils.

In this investigation you will develop a simulation, or model, for the half-life of a radioactive element.

Problem

How can half-life be demonstrated?

Materials *(per group)*

2 500-mL beakers
500 mL of radioactive element X
food coloring
medicine dropper
10-mL graduated cylinder
100-mL graduated cylinder
clock or watch with second hand

Procedure

1. Mark one of the 500-mL beakers A and the other B.
2. Fill beaker A with 500 mL of radioactive element X.
3. Place 5 drops of food coloring in beaker B.
4. Record below the half-life of your group's radioactive element.

   Half-life: ______________________

5. To illustrate each half-life, use the appropriate graduated cylinder to divide the radioactive element in beaker A in half every time a half-life period ends. Pour the portion of the radioactive element that has decayed into beaker B. For example, if the half-life is 30 seconds, every 30 seconds divide the radioactive element in beaker A in half.
6. Follow the decay of your radioactive element through six half-lives. Complete the Data Table as you work.
7. Graph your data on the graph provided in Observations. Be sure to fill in the numbers on the Time Passed (min) axis. Select numbers that are appropriate for your half-life.
8. Report your results to your class.

Observations

DATA TABLE

Half-life period	Time passed (min)	Volume of Beaker A (mL)
0	0	500
1		
2		
3		
4		
5		
6		

GRAPH

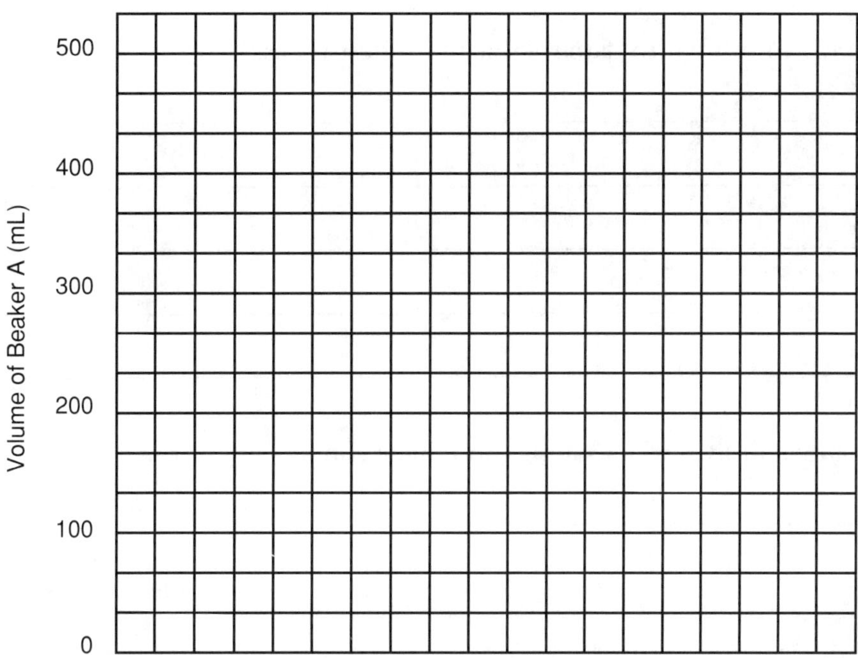

Conclusions

1. Which beaker contained the radioactive element? ______________________

   Decay element? ______________________

2. Do all radioactive elements have the same half-life? ______________________

3. By what amount does the volume in beaker A decrease for each half-life period?

   ____

4. Does the shape of your graph resemble the shapes of graphs of your classmates? Why or why not? ______________________

   ____

   ____

   ____

Critical Thinking and Application

1. Could your radioactive element be used for dating a dinosaur bone? Why or why not?

2. Why is carbon-14 not used to date the Earth's oldest rocks?

3. After how many half-lives will a sample no longer contain any of the radioactive element?

Going Further

The following is known about a fossil bone:

Amount of carbon-14 originally in bone—400 g
Amount of carbon-14 presently in bone—100 g
Amount of carbon-12 presently in bone—300 g

Carbon-12 is the decay element produced when carbon-14 undergoes the process of radioactive decay. Carbon-14 has a half-life of 5770 years.

How old is this fossil bone? ____________________

Explain how you arrived at your answer.

Exploring Geologic Time Through Sediment "Core" Samples

Background Information

One way in which scientists study past life is to examine fossil evidence found in sediment buried beneath the Earth's surface. Over a long period of time, sediment and the remains of organisms have been deposited, layer upon layer. Scientists collect sediment samples containing fossils by driving hollow tubes into sediment layers and withdrawing the tubes with the sediment layers intact. This process is called coring. The resulting core samples showing the various layers of sediment and fossil remains are then examined.

In this investigation you will create sediment deposits and obtain a core sample of these deposits. You will then interpret the sediments contained within the core sample, much as scientists do when they observe geologic evidence.

Problem

How are core samples collected and interpreted?

Materials *(per group)*

1-L milk carton
sediments:
  loose clay or red-colored sand
  white-colored sand
  potting soil or mud
  ground up leaves or grass
2 plastic drinking straws
pencil
paper
metric ruler

Procedure

1. Decide on the type and order of the sediments that will be placed in your empty milk carton. You may use two or more of the sediments. Record your group's sediment order in Observations.
2. Take two or three handfuls of one type of sediment and place them in the bottom of the milk carton. Continue this process, following your sediment order, until the carton is almost full. You may make the sediment layers of different thicknesses.
3. Add enough water to your sediment layers to make them moist.
4. Exchange your carton of sediment layers for a carton prepared by another group of students.

5. Collect a core sample from this sediment container by tightly holding the top of a straw with your fingers and pushing the straw "corer" into the sediments.
6. Gently pull out the straw with the sample from the sediment container. Using a pencil, carefully push the sediment out one end of the straw onto a sheet of paper that is folded in half. The core sample should rest in the fold of the paper.
7. Record the sediments in their correct order in Figure 1 of Observations. Measure the height of each layer in centimeters and place the measurements next to the recorded layers.
8. Check your results with the group that set up the sediment carton.

Observations

Your group's sediment order:

Bottom layer ____

Middle layer(s) ____

Top layer ____

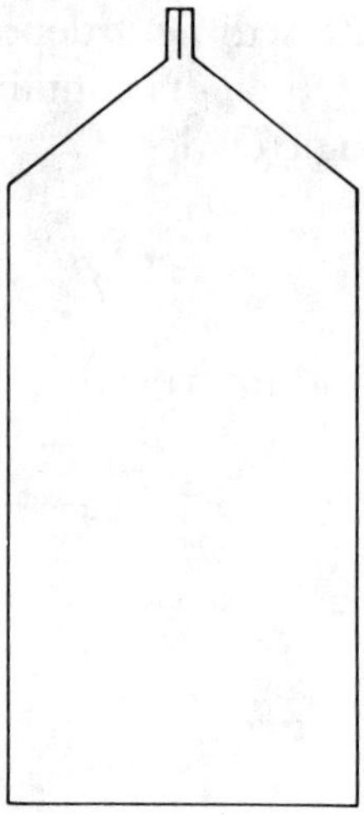

Figure 1

Conclusions

1. Which layer is the oldest?

____

2. Which layer is the youngest?

____

3. What information can scientists find from studying core samples?

____

____

____

Name ______________________ Class ____________ Date ________

Critical Thinking and Application

1. Why should a geologist exercise great care and patience when drilling for a core sample and then removing it? ______________________

____

____

____

2. How might an earthquake affect the way sediments are layered in a core sample?

____

____

____

3. How could a core sample be useful in choosing a site to drill for oil?

____

____

____

Going Further

Choose extinct animals or plants to represent in a fossil exhibit. Research these organisms in the library. Make clay and plaster of Paris fossil models of the organisms you have chosen, or traces of these organisms. For example, you may want to make a fossil model of a dinosaur footprint. You can do this by placing a layer of clay in the bottom of a small cardboard container. Form the shape of the footprint in the clay and coat the clay with petroleum jelly. Pour plaster of Paris into the container so that it is five centimeters thick. When the plaster of Paris has hardened, remove the clay and observe your fossil model of the footprint. For each fossil, prepare an information card that includes the name of the organism and the geologic era in which the organism lived.

Name ______________________ Class ____________ Date ________

Laboratory Investigation

Chapter 21 Energy Resources **46**

Fractional Distillation

Background Information

Fractional distillation is a process by which different liquids combined in a mixture can be separated on the basis of their different boiling points. During the process, the mixture is heated slowly so that each substance, or fraction, in the mixture reaches its boiling point and vaporizes. As it vaporizes, it leaves the liquid and passes to an area where it is cooled and condensed back to its liquid phase. The fraction is now separated from other substances in the mixture. Fractional distillation is used in the petroleum industry to separate crude oil into its many useful parts, which include gasoline, jet fuel, lubricants, and waxes.

In this investigation you will perform a fractional distillation of a mixture of water, isopropyl (“rubbing”) alcohol, and ethylene glycol.

Problem

How can a mixture of liquids be separated by fractional distillation?

Materials *(per group)*

3 large test tubes
ring stand
test-tube clamp
test-tube rack
2-hole rubber stopper (to fit test tube)
400-mL beaker with crushed ice
several boiling chips
right-angle glass tubing
rubber tubing, 40 cm
Bunsen burner
Celsius thermometer
isopropyl alcohol
ethylene glycol
graph paper

Procedure

1. Half-fill a test tube with the liquid mixture provided by your teacher. Put the test tube in the test-tube rack while you set up the apparatus.
2. Set up the apparatus as shown in Figure 1. Note that the bulb of the thermometer is near the top of the test tube, not in the liquid. Place a few boiling chips in the test tube.

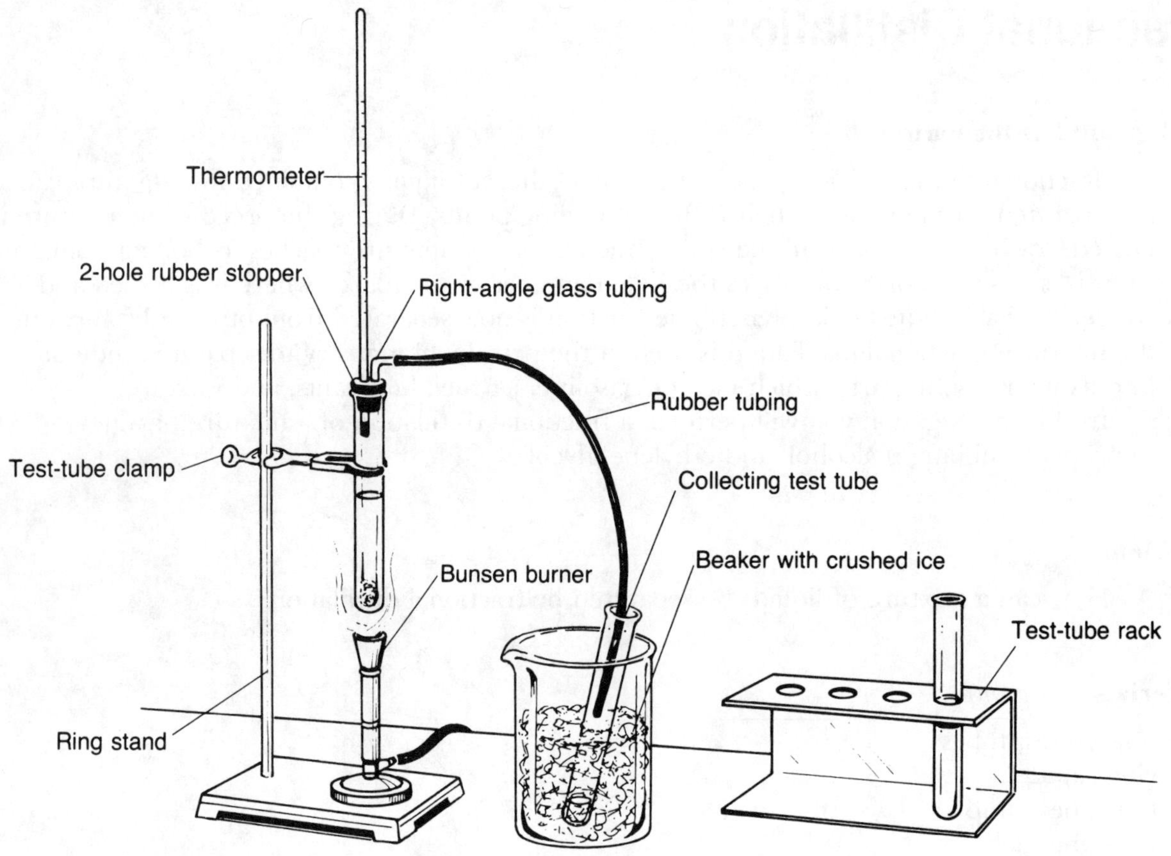

Figure 1

3. Light the Bunsen burner and slowly heat the test tube. Make sure that the flame is a moderate one. Do not allow the liquid to boil rapidly. Record the temperature at one-minute intervals in the Data Table.
4. When the temperature stops rising, you should notice a liquid beginning to collect in the test tube in the beaker of crushed ice. Note this temperature in the Data Table. **CAUTION:** *Do not allow the rubber tubing to touch the liquid being collected.*
5. When the temperature begins rising again, remove the collecting test tube from the crushed ice and replace it with an empty test tube. Place the test tube with the collected liquid in the test-tube rack.
6. When the temperature again stops rising, you should notice a liquid beginning to collect in the test tube. Note this temperature in the Data Table. Do not allow the rubber tubing to touch the liquid being collected.
7. When the temperature begins rising again, turn off the Bunsen burner and allow the heated test tube to cool before taking apart the apparatus.

Name ______________________ Class ____________ Date ________

Observations

DATA TABLE

Time (min)	1	2	3	4	5	6	7	8	9	10	11	12	13	14	15
Temperature (°C)															

1. At what temperature did the first liquid fraction begin to collect in the cool test tube?

____

2. At what temperature did the second liquid fraction begin to collect in the cool test tube? ____

3. Describe the liquid remaining in the heated test tube.

____

4. Carefully smell the separated fractions and describe their odor.

____

____

Analysis and Conclusions

1. Draw a graph of your data. Plot time along the horizontal axis and temperature along the vertical axis.
2. On the basis of your observations of boiling temperature, odor, and appearance, identify the three fractions. ____

____

3. Explain how each liquid was separated and then collected.

____

____

____

____

____

____

Critical Thinking and Application

1. Did the complete separation of liquid fractions take place? ______

   Explain. ______

2. Under what circumstances would it be more difficult to separate the fractions in a liquid mixture? ______

3. How do you know that fractional distillation is a physical separation, not a chemical one? ______

Going Further

Solid substances can also be separated into useful components by a similar process called destructive distillation. Do library research to find out how destructive distillation is accomplished and what kinds of products result.

An Experiment in Hydroponics

Background Information

As the population of the Earth continues to increase, the problem of how to feed all the people becomes more difficult to solve. The reduction of agricultural areas to make room for more housing adds to the problem. One way scientists are trying to solve the problem is by growing plants through hydroponics. Hydroponics is a method of growing plants in nutrient solutions without soil. This method allows farmers to grow plants in many different environments.

In this investigation you will attempt to grow plants in various types of plant-supporting mediums that have been treated with a hydroponic chemical solution.

Problem

In what plant-supporting medium do plants grow best?

Materials *(per group)*

- 3 small flowerpots with drainage openings
- 3 saucers
- plant-supporting mediums: sawdust or straw, sand, and gravel
- hydroponic solution
- graduated cylinder
- metric ruler
- glass-marking pencil
- 6 bean seeds

Procedure

1. Label the flowerpots A, B, and C.
2. In flowerpot A, place 5 cm of gravel. In flowerpot B, place 5 cm of sand. In flowerpot C, place 5 cm of straw or sawdust. The plant-supporting mediums used in the flowerpots are your experimental variables.
3. Plant two bean seeds in each flowerpot, approximately 1.5 cm from the top of the plant-supporting medium.
4. Add 15 mL of hydroponic solution to each flowerpot.
5. Each day, observe the flowerpots and add enough hydroponic solution to keep the plant-supporting medium moist. Keep accurate measurements of the growth of your plants for 2 to 4 weeks. Each day, record the results of your experiment on the Graph. Use the Key next to the Graph when recording your results.

Observations

GRAPH

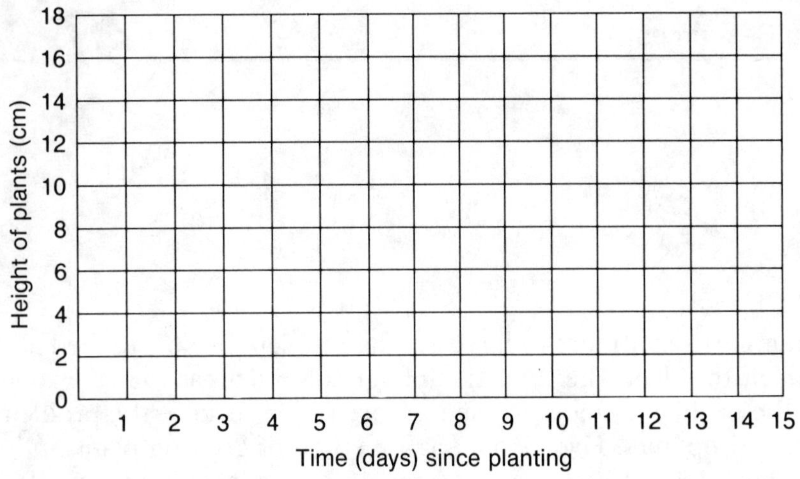

Analysis and Conclusions

1. What is meant by the term hydroponics?

____

____

2. In which type of plant-supporting medium did the bean plant grow largest?

____

____

3. What conclusions can you make concerning the growth of plants in a hydroponic garden? _______________

____

____

____

Critical Thinking and Application

1. How could hydroponic gardening help solve food shortage problems in the future?

____

____

____

2. Are there any disadvantages to hydroponic gardening? Explain.

3. Would plants grown in hydroponic solutions still need light in order to grow? Explain.

Going Further

Find out if soil and hydroponic solutions affect plant growth rate differently. Obtain five different kinds of seeds, six of each kind. Plant three of each kind of seed in soil and three of each kind of seed in a plant-supporting medium in hydroponic solution. Keep a record of the growth rate of each of the seeds and of the general appearance of the plants. Write a report based on your observations. Include a graph of the growth rates.

Investigating the Effects of Pollution on Germination

Background Information

Environmental pollution is becoming an ever-increasing problem. Environmental pollution includes air pollution, water pollution, and land pollution. A cause of air pollution is the burning of fossil fuels such as gasoline, oil, and coal. The pollutants, or harmful and unwanted substances given off when fossil fuels are burned, are released into the air. These pollutants include sulfur and nitrogen compounds and are the major contributors to acid rain. Acid rain forms when water vapor in the air mixes with sulfur and nitrogen compounds called oxides. When the oxides mix with the water vapor, they form droplets of sulfuric and nitric acid. Acid rain that falls on land can damage plant life and the soil. Acid rain that falls into lakes can destroy both plant and animal life.

Detergents in untreated sewage that is dumped into ponds and lakes can cause water pollution. Detergents are chemicals that contain phosphates. Phosphates are nutrients for aquatic plants. When dumped into a lake, phosphates will cause an increased growth of plants such as algae. These plants use up the oxygen supply of the lake. Materials such as salts from mining sites also contribute to water pollution.

In this investigation you will observe the effects of some of these pollutants on the germination of seeds.

Problem

What effects do certain pollutants have on the germination of seeds?

Materials *(per group)*

scissors
blotter paper
plastic sandwich bag
glass-marking pencil
forceps
4 pinto bean seeds that were soaked in water and in solutions of acid, detergent, and salt
medicine dropper
stapler
masking tape

Procedure

1. With scissors, cut a strip of blotter paper 4 cm wide and 16 cm long.
2. With the glass-marking pencil, divide the strip into four equal sections. Label the first section Acid; the second, Detergent; the third, Salt; and the fourth, Control.
3. Place the blotter paper in the bottom of the sandwich bag with the labels facing the back of the bag. See Figure 1.
4. Using forceps, remove a pinto bean seed from each beaker of bean seeds. Place each seed in the corresponding section on the blotter, as shown in Figure 1.
5. With the medicine dropper, thoroughly moisten the blotter paper with water.
6. Carefully fold the bag over the blotter paper and bean seeds. Try not to disturb the beans.
7. With the stapler, place a row of staples between each bean seed to secure the seed within its section.

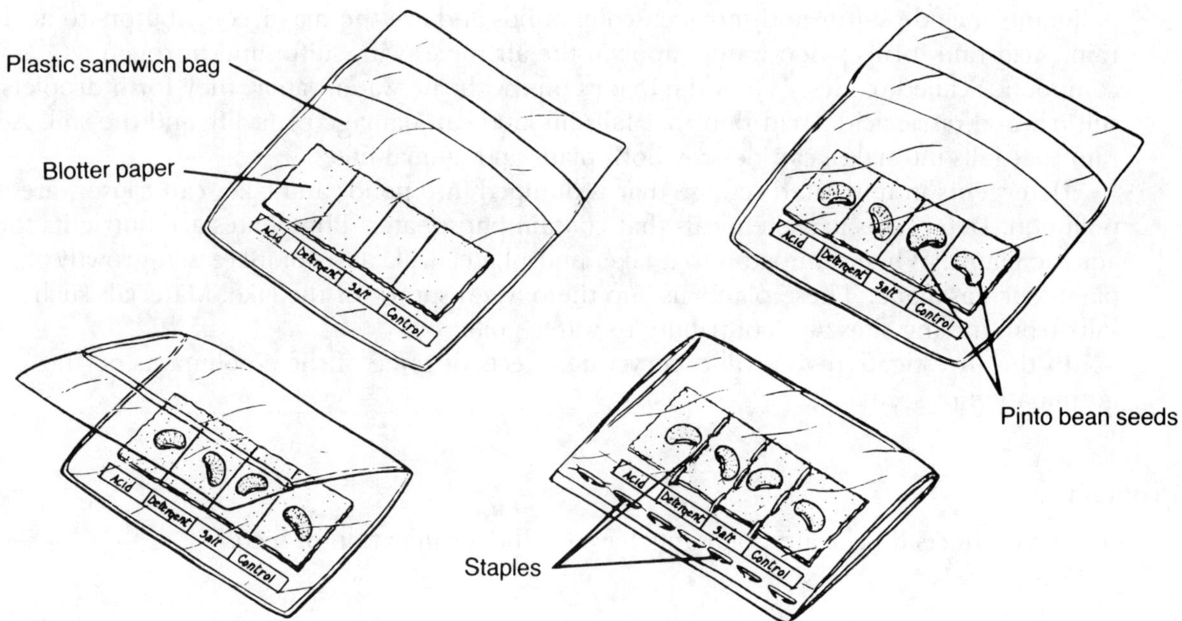

Figure 1

8. Write the name of a group member and your class period on a piece of masking tape. Place the masking tape in a corner of the sandwich bag.
9. Place the sandwich bag in an area where it will not be disturbed for 5 days.
10. Observe the seeds each day for evidence of germination. Record your observations in the Data Table.

Name ______________________ Class ____________ Date ________

Observations

DATA TABLE

Day	Pollutants	Observations
1	Acid	
	Detergent	
	Salt	
	Control	
2	Acid	
	Detergent	
	Salt	
	Control	
3	Acid	
	Detergent	
	Salt	
	Control	
4	Acid	
	Detergent	
	Salt	
	Control	
5	Acid	
	Detergent	
	Salt	
	Control	

Analysis and Conclusions

1. What source of pollution does each pollutant in the investigation represent?

a. Acid ______________________

b. Detergent ______________________

c. Salt ______________________

2. Why do you need a control? ____

____

3. Explain why the "control" seed was placed in the same sandwich bag as the other seeds and not in a separate bag. ____

____

____

____

Critical Thinking and Application

1. Why is it necessary to observe the seeds over a 5-day period?

____

____

____

2. A farmer has recently sprayed his crops with an insecticide. Soon after, fishes in a nearby pond begin to die. Explain how the actions of the farmer may have resulted in the death of the fishes. ____

____

____

____

____

____

____

Going Further

Repeat this investigation using different pollutants. Compare the results of this investigation with the results of the original investigation.

Laboratory Investigation

Chapter 23 Pollution **49**

The Greenhouse Effect

Background Information

Most pollutants in the atmosphere are easily detected. Smoke, sulfur oxides, dust and dirt particles, and ozone are not normal components of the atmosphere and their presence is quickly and easily recognized. Carbon dioxide gas, however, is not so easily detected. This odorless, tasteless, and colorless gas is normally a part of the atmosphere. Usually present as only 0.03 percent of the atmosphere, the amount of carbon dioxide is steadily increasing as a result of the increased burning of fossil fuels for energy.

Carbon dioxide in the atmosphere acts much like the glass in a greenhouse to trap heat. So scientists are predicting that a steady increase in the amount of atmospheric carbon dioxide will result in an overall warming of the Earth. Such a warming could in turn lead to a melting of the polar icecaps, a rise in sea level, and a flooding of many coastal and low-lying areas.

In this investigation you will explore the greenhouse effect and explain its impact on our atmosphere.

Problem

What is the greenhouse effect?

Materials *(per group)*

small jar with cover
2 Celsius thermometers with plastic or metal backing
dark soil
lamp
ring stand
2 test-tube clamps
triple-beam balance
weighing paper

Procedure

1. Use the balance to obtain a 25-g sample of soil. Place it in the small jar.
2. Insert the thermometer into the slit that has been precut in the jar lid.
3. Place the cover on the jar. Lay the jar on its side on the table. Attach the test-tube clamp, which is already attached to the ring stand, to the thermometer to hold it in place. Be sure that the soil does not touch the thermometer.
4. Measure out another 25-g sample of soil on a piece of weighing paper.
5. Attach the other test-tube clamp, which is also attached to the ring stand, to the second thermometer. Place the 25-g sample of soil on its piece of paper under the thermometer.
6. Adjust the light so that it is the same distance from both thermometers. A good distance is about 30 cm.

7. Record the starting temperature of each thermometer in the Data Table. Then record the temperature every minute for 10 minutes.

8. Turn off the light and record the temperature of each thermometer again every minute for 10 minutes.

Observations

DATA TABLE

	Time	Temperature of Air in Jar (°C)	Temperature of Air Outside Jar (°C)
Light on	0		
	1		
	2		
	3		
	4		
	5		
	6		
	7		
	8		
	9		
	10		
Light off	11		
	12		
	13		
	14		
	15		
	16		
	17		
	18		
	19		
	20		

Name ______________________ Class ____________ Date ________

Analysis and Conclusions

1. Which of the two thermometers recorded the greater increase in temperature?

   ____

   Why? ____

   ____

2. Which of the two thermometers recorded the greater decrease in temperature?

   ____

   Why? ____

   ____

3. What part of the atmosphere is represented by the glass jar?

   ____

4. Explain why a cloudy night is usually warmer than a clear night.

   ____

   ____

5. Why was soil placed under the thermometer that was in the air?

   ____

   ____

   ____

Critical Thinking and Application

1. Explain how a greenhouse traps heat. ______________________

   ____

   ____

   ____

   ____

   ____

   ____

2. Explain how the atmosphere acts like the glass in a greenhouse.

3. Why does the amount of carbon dioxide in the atmosphere remain virtually the same as long as humans do not interfere?

4. Predict some of the consequences of a continued warming trend for the Earth.

5. Not all scientists agree that the Earth will continue to warm up. Some predict a "steady state," whereas others predict a cooling trend and perhaps another ice age. State an argument in favor of each of these predictions.

Going Further

Research the possible long-term consequences of the addition of other air pollutants to our atmosphere.

Name ______________________ Class __________ Date ________

Laboratory Investigation

Chapter 23 Pollution **50**

Observing Oil Spills

Background Information

The need for fossil fuels, such as coal and oil, is very important to people. These fuels must be transported from where they are removed from the Earth to where they are refined and from there to where they are needed. In recent years, there have been a number of accidents in which oil tankers have lost their cargoes while at sea. Oil spills have an effect on the ecology of the ocean.

In this investigation you will duplicate some of the processes at work when an accident causes an oil spill.

Problem

How can you demonstrate the effects of oil spills on a seashore?

Materials *(per class)*

stream table
thin metal sheet or piece of wood (15 cm × 30 cm × 1 cm)
25 mL of vegetable oil
feather
liquid detergent
4 to 8 wooden popsicle sticks

Procedure

1. Set up the stream table on a flat and level surface. Seal the drainage hole. See Figure 1.

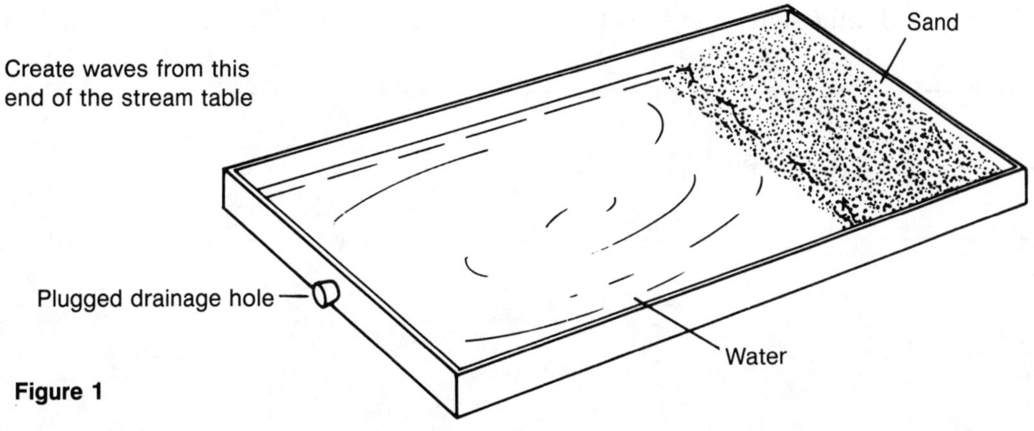

Figure 1

2. Use fine sand only and create a model of a beach. The sand should cover only one fourth of the total area of the stream table and be about 3 cm deep. Carefully fill the remaining three fourths of the table with water.
3. Use the thin metal sheet or wood to make waves. At the end of the table opposite the "beach," quickly dip the edge of the metal sheet or wood into the water and then lift it out. Keep repeating this motion approximately once every 1 or 2 seconds.
4. At a position about 5 cm in front of where the waves are being made, carefully pour 25 mL of vegetable oil into the water.
5. Observe how the oil behaves in the water.
6. As the "oil spill" spreads out, carefully stick your finger into the center. Notice what happens when you remove your finger.
7. Insert the feather into the "oil spill." Notice what happens.
8. Try to find a way to prevent the "spill" from reaching the "beach." One method is to use liquid detergents to break up the oil. Use some liquid detergent on one portion of the oil. Observe what happens. Another method is to try to contain the spill with floats to prevent the spill from traveling. Use the popsicle sticks to try to prevent the oil from reaching the "beach." Observe what happens. You may want to think of other methods that could be tried. Discuss your ideas with the class.

Observations

1. How does the oil spill behave in the water? ____________________

____

2. What happens to objects such as your finger or the feather when they are dipped into the oil in the water? ____________________

____

3. How is the feather changed by the contact with the oil?

____

____

4. What effect did the liquid detergent have when it came in contact with the oil?

____

5. What effect did the stick floats have on the oil spill?

____

Name ______________________________ Class ______________ Date __________

Analysis and Conclusions

1. How is your model similar to a real oil spill? ______________________________

2. How is your model different from a real oil spill?

3. How would a bird be affected by contact with a real oil spill?

4. What do you think would happen to other life forms that came in contact with an oil spill? ______________________________

5. Based on your observations, list two techniques that might be useful in cleaning up an ocean oil spill. ______________________________

Critical Thinking and Application

1. How might the tourist industry of certain coastal areas be affected when oil spills occur close to shore? ______________________________

2. How might the fishing industry of a community be affected by an oil spill?

____

____

____

3. What other energy resources are now being used in an attempt to decrease our dependence on fossil fuels? ____

____

____

____

4. In addition to large tankers, what else is sometimes responsible for creating oil spills in the ocean? ____

____

____

Going Further

Investigate the effects of oil on sand and plants. Add some oil to some beach sand. After the sand has been mixed with oil, try to clean it using some liquid detergent. Immerse the leaves and stems of some plants in oil. Plant them in soil and let them grow. How well do they grow? Is it possible for normal forces such as wind and rain to cleanse them? Record your observations over several days or weeks.

Name ______________________ Class __________ Date ________

Laboratory Investigation

Chapter 23 Pollution **51**

Treating Polluted Water

Background Information

Today, raw sewage must be treated before it is allowed to enter our rivers, lakes, and oceans. Polluted water is usually treated in three steps. First, the water is exposed to oxygen, or aerated, by stirring or bubbling air through the liquid. This causes harmful organic pollutants to react with oxygen and change to harmless water and carbon dioxide. The water is next allowed to filter down through layers of sand and gravel. Finally, chlorine is added to kill any remaining harmful organic matter.

In this investigation you will treat polluted water using the three basic steps.

Problem

How is polluted water treated so that it does not harm our rivers, lakes, and oceans?

Materials *(per group)*

sand
fine gravel
medium gravel
funnel
filter paper
ring stand and ring
aerator or stirrer
chlorine
large jar
4 large test tubes
test-tube rack
2 400-mL beakers
green food coloring
soil
organic matter
detergent
glass-marking pencil

Procedure

1. Fill a large jar or milk container three-fourths full of water. Add some soil, ground-up organic matter such as grass clippings or orange peels, a small amount of detergent, and a few drops of green food coloring.
2. Cap the jar, shake it well, and let the mixture stand in the sun.
3. After your polluted sample has "ripened" for a day or two, shake the mixture and pour a sample into one of the test tubes. Label this test tube Before Treatment.
4. Use an aerator from an aquarium to bubble air through your sewage in the jar. You should allow several hours for aeration; leave the aerator attached overnight if possible. If you do not have an aerator, use a mechanical stirrer or mixer.
5. When aeration is complete, pour another sample into a second test tube labeled Aerated Sample.
6. Fold a piece of filter paper in half. Now fold it in half once more, so you have a quarter of a pie. Hold three sides together and pull out the remaining side to form a cone. Wet the paper with tap water and then insert the cone in a funnel. Mount the funnel on a ring stand.

7. Place a layer of medium gravel, then fine gravel, and finally white sand in the funnel, as shown in Figure 1. A filtration plant does not use filter paper, but the sand trap is several meters deep. The paper replaces several layers of sand.

8. Pour the remaining aerated liquid through the filter. Do not allow the liquid to spill over the filter paper. You may have to filter the same liquid several times before you obtain good results.

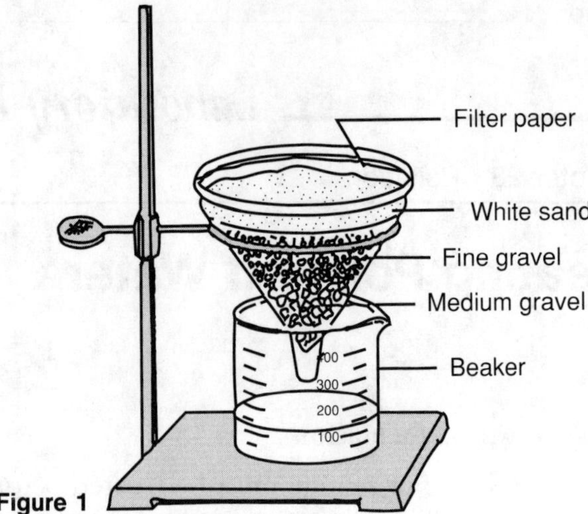

Figure 1

9. Pour a sample of the filtered water into a third test tube labeled Filtered.

10. Pour another sample of the filtered water into a fourth test tube labeled Chlorinated. Add a small amount of chlorine to this test tube. Mix well until the water is clear.

11. Carefully observe all four test tubes. Write a detailed description of each liquid in the Data Table. Include the odor of each sample. **CAUTION:** *Do not taste the water!*

Observations

DATA TABLE

Water Sample	Description
Before Treatment	
Aerated Sample	
Filtered	
Chlorinated	

1. What changes in the composition of the liquid did you observe after aeration?

____

2. Did aeration remove any of the odor? _______________________

3. What was removed by the sand filter? _______________________

4. Did the addition of chlorine cause the water to become clearer?

____

5. Did the chlorine remove the green color? ______________________

Analysis and Conclusions

1. How is your model similar to a real sewage-treatment plant?

____

____

2. How is your model different from a real sewage-treatment plant?

____

____

3. Besides changing the color of polluted water, what other important function does chlorine serve? ______________________________

____

____

4. Why is it important that raw sewage be treated?

____

____

Critical Thinking and Application

1. Of the three types of material you used for filtering—sand, fine gravel, and medium gravel—which one do you think filtered out the most particles from the polluted water?

Explain your answer. ______________________________

____

____

____

2. As the Earth's population increases, water conservation is becoming increasingly important. What things can you do at home to conserve water?

3. How can some of the rich organic materials that are filtered out of raw sewage be of benefit to farmers?

4. Some smaller communities get their water from underground wells. Why would it be wise for community members to replace their systems of individual, underground sewage-holding tanks with a sewage system that carries raw sewage away to a large sewage-treatment plant?

Going Further

1. Add detergent to the polluted water; then filter and chlorinate the water. Is the detergent completely removed?
2. Home water purifiers use activated charcoal to trap pollutants. Try adding some activated charcoal between the sand and gravel and filtering some of the polluted water. Can you observe a difference from the sample filtered without charcoal?

Should You Take a Bath or a Shower?

Background Information

Fresh water is one of our most precious natural resources. Although water is a renewable natural resource, most of the Earth's water is in the ocean. Ocean water is not suitable for many human activities because it contains salt.

It is estimated that each person in the United States uses about 400 L of water every day for drinking, bathing, cleaning, and cooking. In order to have enough usable water constantly available, it is important to conserve water. Recent water shortages have convinced many people that water is not limitless! People can help conserve water in many ways.

In this investigation you will compare the quantity of water used in taking a shower and a bath. Then you will be better able to make decisions about conserving water.

Problem

Which requires less water: a bath or a shower?

Materials *(per student)*

metric ruler
bathtub with shower

Procedure

Part A Bath

1. Run your bath water.
2. Before getting into the tub, measure the depth of the water with the metric ruler.
3. Record the depth of the water in the Data Table.

Part B Shower

1. Close the bathtub drain.
2. Take a shower.
3. Before draining the bathtub, measure the depth of the water with the metric ruler. **Note:** *Do not stand in the tub when measuring the depth of the water.*
4. Record the depth of the water in the Data Table.

Observations

I usually take a ______________________________.

DATA TABLE

	Depth of water
Bath	
Shower	

Analysis and Conclusions

1. Does a bath or a shower require more water? ______________________________

2. Should the procedure have included a specific length of time for your shower?

3. Why is it important that the depth of the water in the tub be measured with you not in the tub? ______________________________

Critical Thinking and Application

1. Explain why water is considered a renewable resource.

2. Would it be a practical solution to water shortages to use fresh water for drinking and cooking only and to use ocean water for industry and agriculture? Explain.

Name ______________________________ Class ______________ Date __________

3. Describe a procedure that would make ocean water usable for drinking and cooking purposes. ______________________________

____

____

____

____

4. Why is it important to conserve our water supply? To keep it unpolluted?

____

____

____

____

5. Using the graphs below, draw a conclusion about the importance of conservation of the Earth's natural resources.

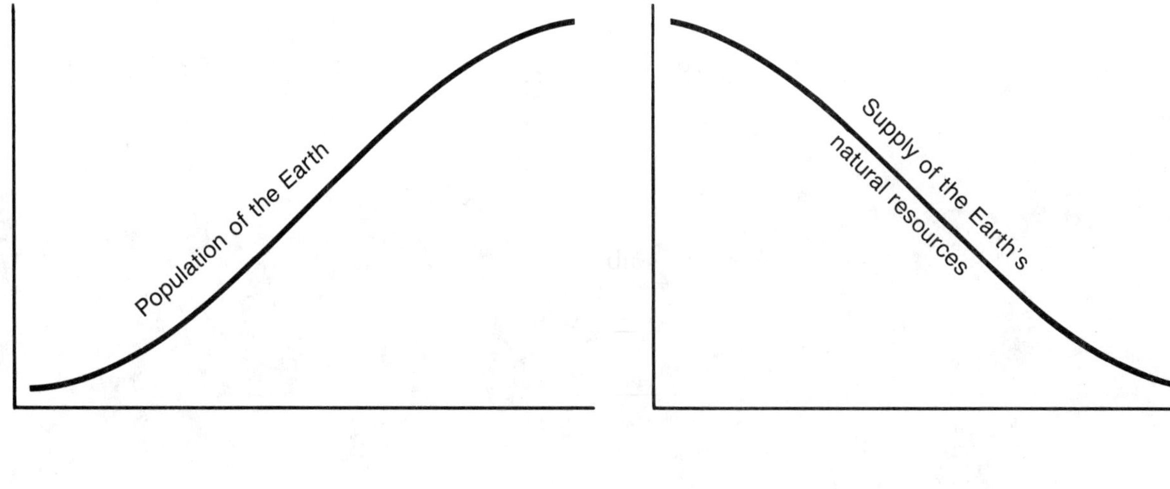

____

____

____

Going Further

1. Your city is experiencing a severe water shortage. As a citizen, list ways in which you can conserve water during this crisis.

2. Using the formula for volume, $V = L \times W \times H$, determine how much water you use in a year to bathe or shower.